The Catholic Home Gallery

Eighteen Works of Art by Contemporary Catholic Artists—Removeable and suitable for framing

Edited by
John Herreid

Foreword by
Emily Stimpson Chapman

IGNATIUS

Cover art:
St. Scholastica, © Gwyneth Thompson-Briggs
Mary Star of the Sea, © Bernadette Carstensen
Saint Padre Pio, © Matthew Conner
Saint Charles Lwanga, © Neilson Carlin
Blessed Solanus Casey, © Matthew Alderman
Miracle of the Sun, © James B. Janknegt
The Assumption of the Blessed Virgin Mary,
© Michael D. O'Brien
Mary, Queen of Heaven, © Timothy Jones
Servant of God Father Emil Kapaun,
© Elizabeth Zelasko

Cover design by John Herreid

ISBN 978-1-62164-549-8

Printed in Canada

"Looking at icons, and in general at the great masterpieces of Christian art, leads us on an interior way, a way of transcendence, and this brings us, in this purification of the heart, face to face with beauty, or at least a ray of it. In this way it brings us into contact with the power of the truth. I have often said that I am convinced that the true apologetics for the Christian message, the most persuasive proof of its truth, offsetting everything that may appear negative, are the saints, on the one hand, and the beauty that the faith has generated, on the other. For the faith to grow today, we must lead ourselves and the persons we meet to encounter the saints and to come in contact with the beautiful."

—**Joseph Ratzinger**
(**Pope Emeritus Benedict XVI**),
From his book *On the Way to Jesus Christ*

Foreword

By Emily Stimpson Chapman

Our nursery, where each of our three babies has slept, is on the second floor of our old Victorian house. Over the past four years, ever since our first son was born, I have carried one baby after another out from that nursery, into the hallway, and down the stairs toward the entry hall below. I have done this more times than I can count.

Also more times than I can count, I have paused with one of those babies halfway down, on the landing where the staircase turns. I pause at the babies' initiative, not mine, letting them rest their hands on the object they've been looking at since we began our descent: an old stained-glass window, almost as tall as I am.

Our babies first notice the window at around four months of age. As soon as they wake from their sleepy newborn coma, that image of a torch, pieced together in pink, purple, blue, green, and yellow glass, captures their attention. They stare at it, reach for it, pat it, and laugh at it. Before they even recognize their own names, they recognize that the window is special. They see something in it that draws them to it. They see beauty, of course. But also, I think, they see God.

A Window

Six years ago, when my husband and I bought our old house and began fixing her up, I wasn't thinking about children seeing God in a stained-glass window. We were newly married and wanting to start a family, but other than not cluttering up low-lying surfaces with breakable objects, I wasn't designing or decorating with babies in mind. I was decorating with me in mind.

The colors I painted the walls, the salvaged materials I installed (like the stained-glass window), and the art I hung throughout the house—all those decisions were based on what I found beautiful, what comforted me, inspired me, or moved me to pray. I didn't think about how those things would affect future children—at least not during their baby years. I assumed that such things would go unnoticed by my children until they were older.

Those trips down the stairway, past the stained glass, disabused me of that notion quickly. So did the quiet that would come over our first son, Toby, when his eyes would fall on the charcoal sketch of the nursing Virgin in our dining room or the old German oil painting in our living room. I learned that when Toby fussed, one of the easiest ways to calm him was to slowly walk him from painting to painting and talk to him about each work of art.

"Look at the children playing", I would say. Or, "Do you see Jesus' mommy?" I would ask.

Toby's gaze would follow my pointing finger, steady, attentive, full of wonder.

I have long believed, with the Church, that beauty is a window through which we see God. It gives us a glimpse of the order, harmony, and peace for which we were made. Or, more accurately, it gives us a glimpse of the One who is Order, Harmony, and Peace. This is one reason why Catholics used to build beautiful churches and fill them with sacred images in marble, glass, and oil: so that everyone could encounter God through beauty and be formed by that encounter.

I still believe that. Since becoming a mother, however, I have come to see that that it doesn't take age and maturity to encounter God through beauty. Even the youngest of children can perceive God in both the works of His hands and the works of our hands. Which is why I now do think about the babies when I'm decorating. I want our home to do for our children what ancient churches have long done for the faithful: bear witness to God through beauty.

A Teacher

Beauty matters. It's not the most important thing. It's not the only thing. We shouldn't make an idol of it or go broke pursuing it. A beautiful home not animated by love in word and deed is a poor witness to the God who is beauty. But still, beauty matters. It teaches. It forms. It inspires. It delights. And as it does all that, it reminds us of the home for which we were made and of the One who is preparing that home for us.

Fortunately, the making of a beautiful home here on earth is much easier than the executives at HGTV would have us believe. Opening up curtains and blinds to let light flood a space can do wonders for any room. Sweeping the corners, dusting the furniture, and placing a vase of fresh wildflowers on the counter also help. So, too, does hanging beautiful art—even if that art is just a framed print of the Virgin Mary ripped from an old calendar . . . or this book.

Art doesn't have to be sacred art to be beautiful. And every piece of art hung in a Catholic home doesn't have to be explicitly Catholic. At the same time, including beautiful works of sacred art in our home is an important part of creating a beautiful home—the kind of home that forms the souls of saints.

Hanging pictures of Jesus' Life, Passion, and Death on our walls can be an invitation to prayer, helping us lift our hearts to God as we lift our eyes to images of Him.

Resting statues of Saint Anne and Saint Joseph on our living room shelves or mantles can remind us that we are never alone, that a great cloud of witnesses surrounds us, praying for us, guiding us, cheering us on.

Sketches of saints from near and far in the dining room can be a teaching tool—a chance to tell stories of God's holy ones, reflect on the family of God, and remind us of God's saving love.

Images of the Sacred and Immaculate Heart in our bedrooms can be an act of defiance, an insistence on choosing hope even in the face of great loss.

Sturdy crucifixes over doorways can be a declaration that we do not belong to the father of lies, but to the God who is Beauty. We are made in His image.

And all of it together can form the souls of those who dwell in our homes, opening our hearts to God's love, helping us grasp our own dignity, and imparting to us a supernatural world view. With grace, that formation will stay with us always, even as we grow, change, and wander, always calling us back to Beauty, back to Love, back to Home.

The book you are holding in your hands is meant to help you fill your home with that kind of art.

A Tool

In these pages, you will find sacred images created by nine contemporary artists who are continuing the Church's great tradition of sacred art. Through their work, they remind us that creating great Catholic art is not just a thing of the past. It is a thing of the present, an ongoing act of worship and evangelization, a continual witness to the God who is with us.

One goal of this book is to introduce you to their work, which is fine and worthy of both admiration and contemplation.

The second goal is to make it easier for you to bring great Catholic art into your home.

The work these artists have crafted is not only meant to hang in churches. It is meant to hang in homes, where those works of art can come alive, teaching, forming, loving, and evangelizing our families. The artists featured here have generously granted permission to Ignatius Press to perforate the pages of the prints included. This will allow you to pull the prints out of the book and place them into frames and onto walls. There, they can help shape the story of your family, becoming a part of your mission to grow in faith and love together.

Not so much a third goal, but perhaps a third hope, is that these pictures will inspire your family to continue investing in the work of Catholic artists, looking for ways to support them as they carry on the important work of rendering sacred truths on canvas and in stone. Their art is a service to the whole Church and worthy of our patronage, whether that patronage is buying a downloadable print through social media, commissioning a personal piece of sacred art for your home, or supporting your parish in its efforts to bring more beautiful art through its doors.

Regardless of how you choose to use this book, though—for discussion, reflection, prayer, education, or decoration—our greatest hope is that it will draw you and your family closer to the God who is, in some way, reflected in every page and every image. God wants you to know Him. He wants you to see Him. He wants you to delight in Him. He is waiting for you, in paintings and stained-glass windows, in books and statues, in oceans and sunsets. And always and above all, in the Eucharist.

Go to Him.

Table of Contents

Matthew Alderman

MATTHEW ALDERMAN says he grew up surrounded by art. "My parents are great connoisseurs and collectors, and our vacations together were and still are often spent largely in art museums or historic churches. My mother has painted in the past; my grandmother was a prolific amateur painter, and her mother in turn studied at Cuba's national arts academy." A love of drawing led to studying architecture at Notre Dame, and Alderman now divides his time between architectural design for churches and illustration and fine art.

In addition to his architectural and fine art work, Matthew Alderman has written and lectured on the topic in venues such as *First Things*, *Dappled Things*, *St. Austin Review*, on the radio, and at various conferences. He is also a Knight of Magistral Grace in the Order of Malta and a knight of the Equestrian Order of the Holy Sepulchre of Jerusalem. An expert in heraldry, he is an artist for the Committee on Heraldry of the New England Historic Genealogical Society, Boston, Mass., and provided heraldic illustrations for the covers of *Continental Ambitions* and *Continental Achievement*, two books on the Catholic colonial experience in America by the historian Kevin Starr.

"The stereotypical contemporary view of art—which I think has pretty much murdered any good in it—sees it largely as a regurgitation of the artist's interior self-expression. I think I have some private insights to bring to the table as part of the process, but my mission is to depict and express God and His saints in line with what has been passed down to us, through Divine Revelation, through the two millennia of liturgy, art, and Catholic culture."

— **Matthew Alderman**

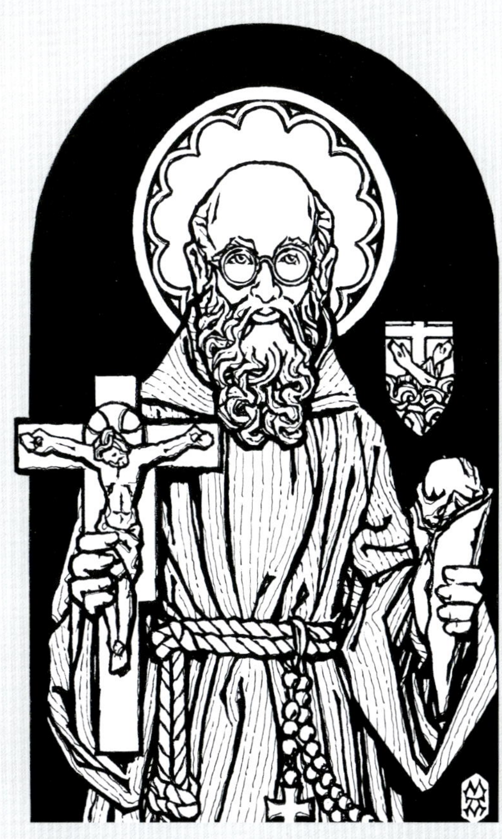

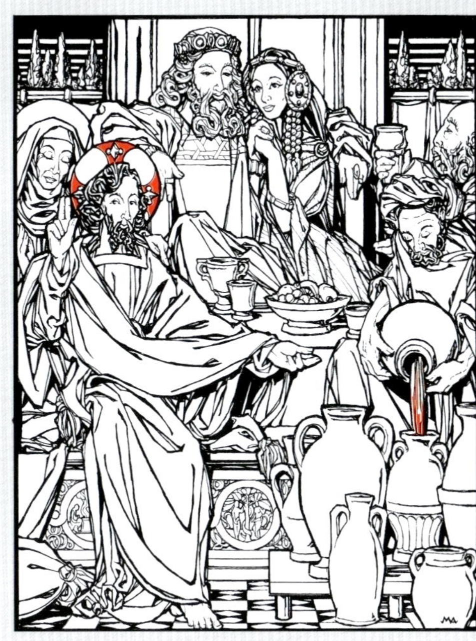

Artist's notes:

Blessed Solanus Casey, 2017
Ink on Architectural Vellum
Private Collection, Canada

Commissioned by a group of friends as a gift to a new mother, Blessed Solanus (1870–1957) is depicted here in his Capuchin friar's habit, holding a crucifix in one hand and an ice cream cone in the other. Inspired by the distinctive and vivid symbols seen in traditional depictions of saints, the artist wished to give to this modern holy figure an equally memorable emblem beyond mere portraiture with which to identify him, here drawn from the well-attested story that the pious if eccentric porter miraculously kept frozen two ice cream cones he had been given by a passing visitor, producing them still cold some hours later from his desk drawer as an impromptu celebration with one of the other friars.

The Wedding at Cana, 2019
Ink on Architectural Vellum
Private Collection, United States

Commissioned for the holy card of a priest's first Mass, this image of the first miracle of Christ's public ministry is inspired stylistically in part by Jewish Art Nouveau illustrator Ephraim Moses Lilien. At the center are the groom with the bride reclining on his chest, with Our Lady leaning in to whisper to her Son "They have no wine" in the foreground. Below, on the bench on which Christ is seated, are small scenes of Adam and Eve and the tree and of the sacrifice of Abel, tying together the nuptial and eucharistic aspects of our redemption. At the right, the steward tests, with astonishment, the new wine.

Matthew Alderman Studios can be found online:

www.matthewalderman.com
Facebook: @matthewaldermanstudios
www.zazzle.com/store/matthewalderman

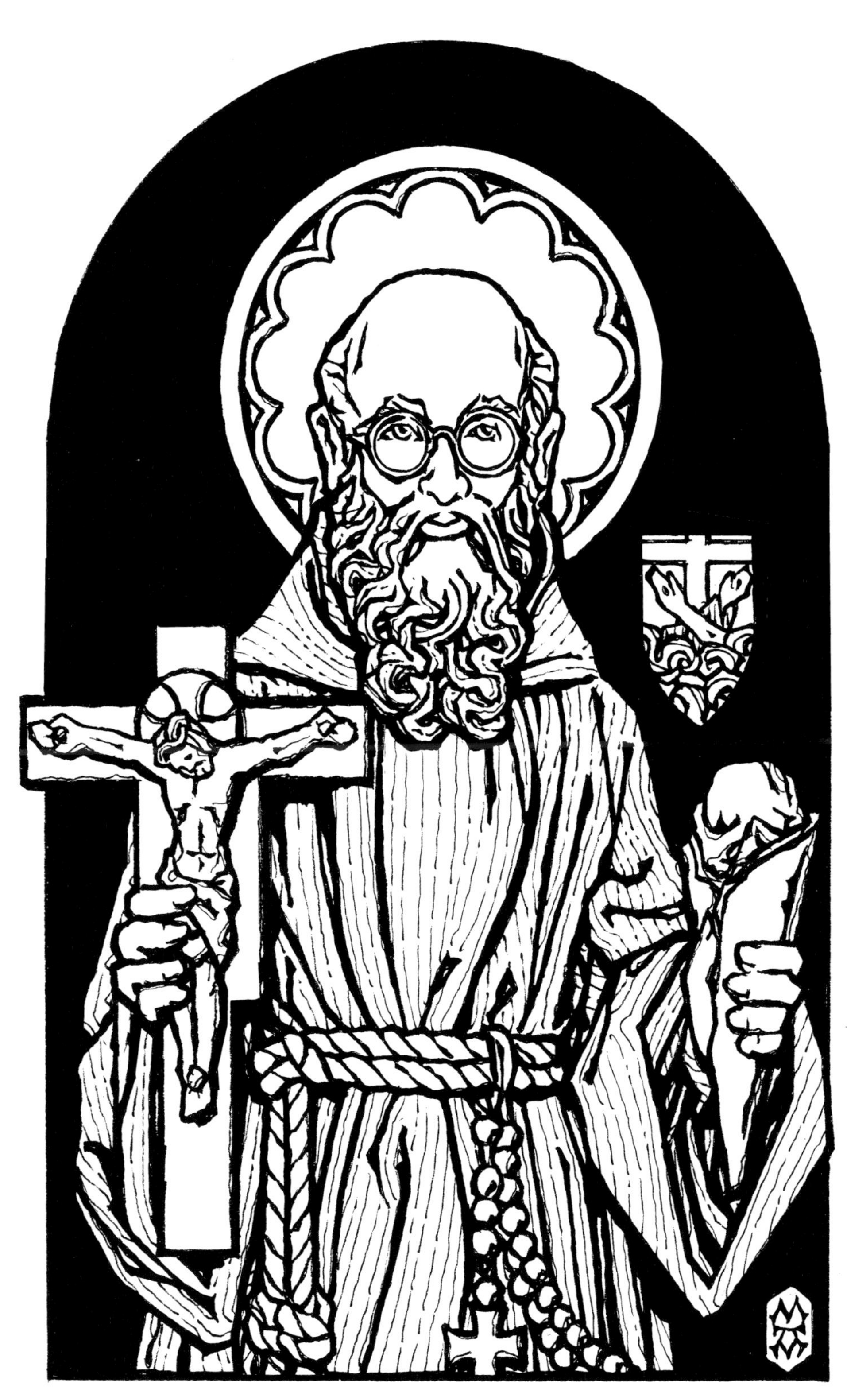

Matthew Alderman, *Blessed Solanus Casey,* 2017
Ink on Architectural Vellum
Private Collection, Canada

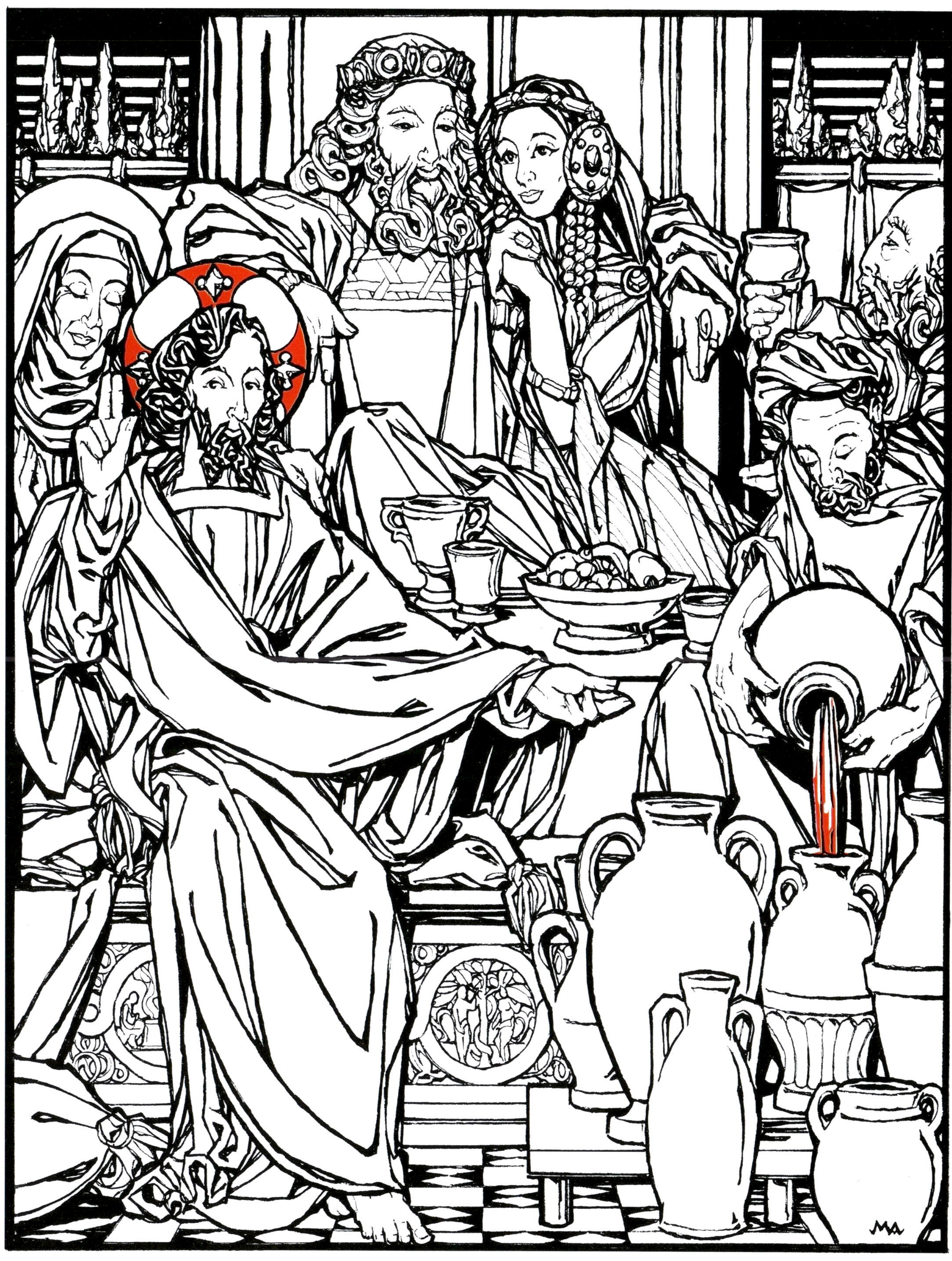

Matthew Alderman, *The Wedding at Cana,* 2019
Ink on Architectural Vellum
Private Collection, United States

Neilson Carlin

"I WENT OFF TO COLLEGE with the sole intent of illustrating for Marvel comics. All these years later, I'm only slightly off the mark. Instead of spending my days drawing heroes of the imagination, I paint the real heroes of the faith", says Neilson Carlin. Educated at the University of the Arts in Philadelphia as well as privately under figure painter Michael Aviano, Neilson traces his instructional lineage back to the École des Beaux-Arts of nineteenth-century France.

Specializing in sacred and devotional art, Neilson's work can be seen at the Shrine of Our Lady of Guadalupe in La Crosse, Wisconsin, as well as other churches and cathedrals around the country. In 2015, he was commissioned by the Archdiocese of Philadelphia to paint the official image of the Holy Family for the World Meeting of Families.

Neilson is also an art teacher. For the past twenty-five years, he has instructed the next generation of artists at his school, the Carlin Academy of Fine Art in Kennett Square, Pennsylvania.

"My faith is indispensable to my image making. When I was in the illustration and secular gallery markets, art was my job. It was a job I thoroughly loved, but I was never emotionally invested in the images I was producing. Bringing the heroes of the faith to life isn't just a job, it's my true calling, my vocation."

— **Neilson Carlin**

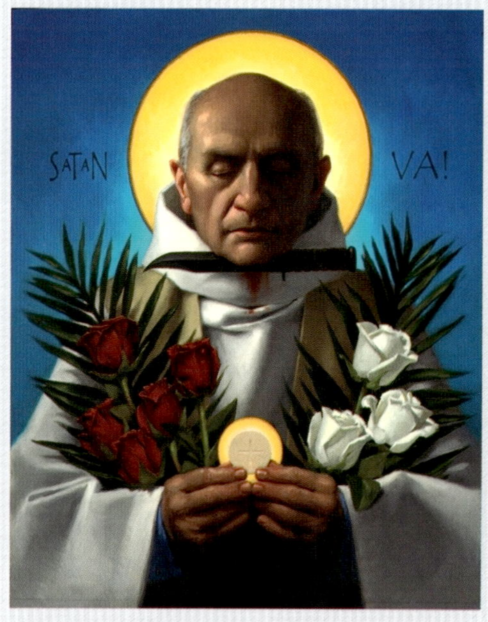

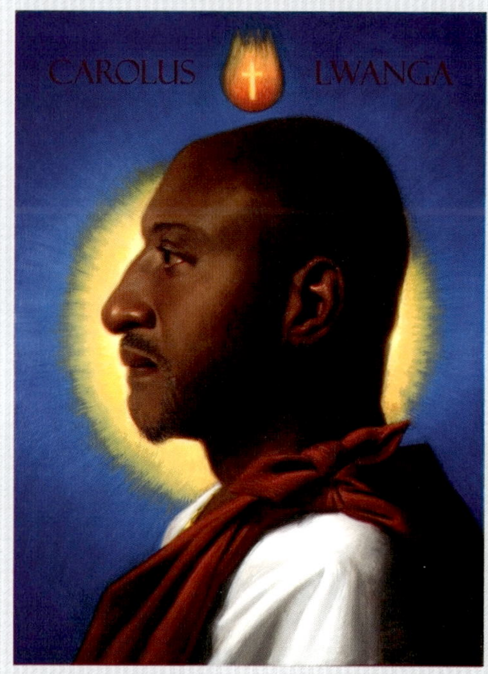

Artist's notes:

Father Jacques Hamel

There are times when the creative process comes quickly, and other times when it is grueling and slow. In the case of Father Hamel, the courage he exhibited at the time of his death inspired me immediately. The design for this piece crystalized in my head within days of hearing about his martyrdom. The imagery is intentionally shocking to remind the viewer about his last minutes and the suffering he endured for his faith.

Saint Charles Lwanga

As an adult Catholic convert without the benefit of parochial schooling, I am always discovering saints as I research and prepare for projects. I am constantly amazed at the faith of the martyrs and, upon hearing the story of Saint Charles and his companions, was moved to create the icon.

You can find Neilson Carlin's work online and at his school, the Carlin Academy of Fine Art:

www.neilsoncarlin.com
www.carlinacademy.com

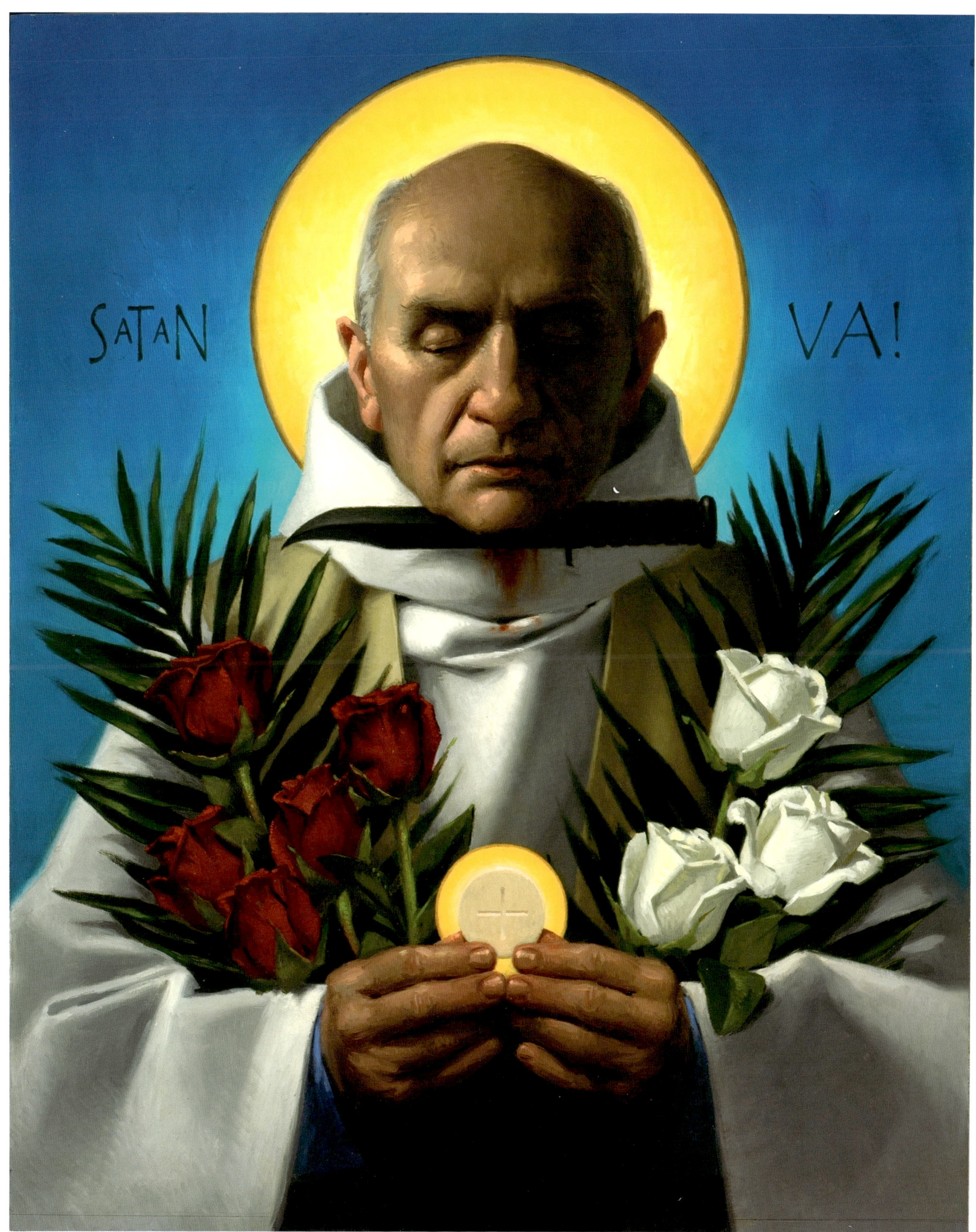
SATAN
VA!

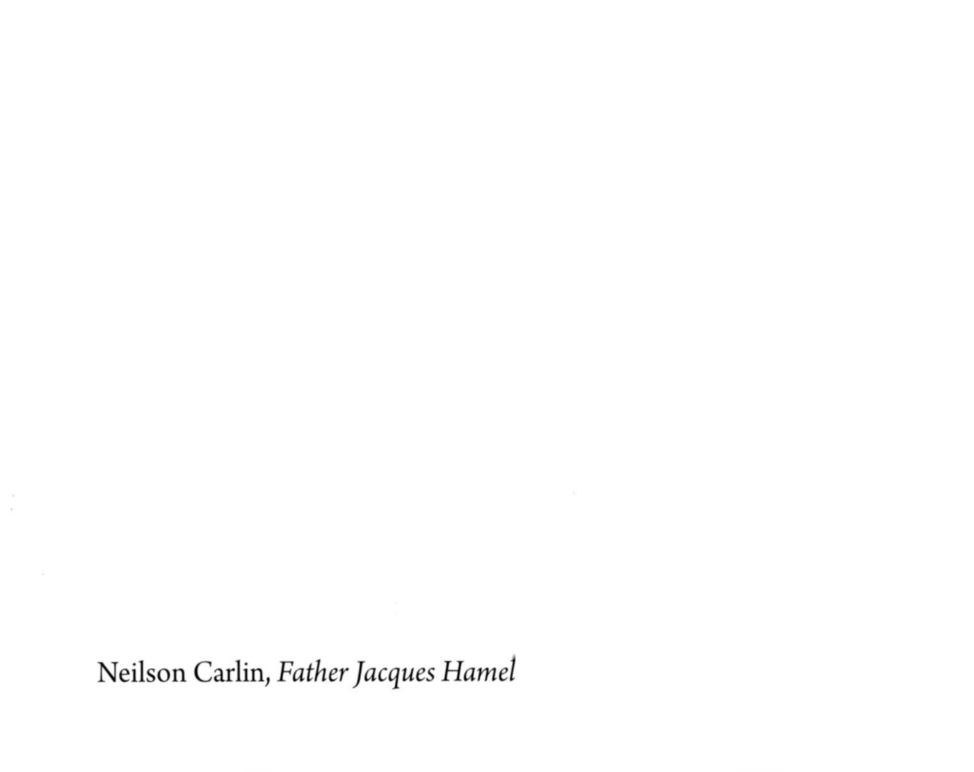

Neilson Carlin, *Father Jacques Hamel*

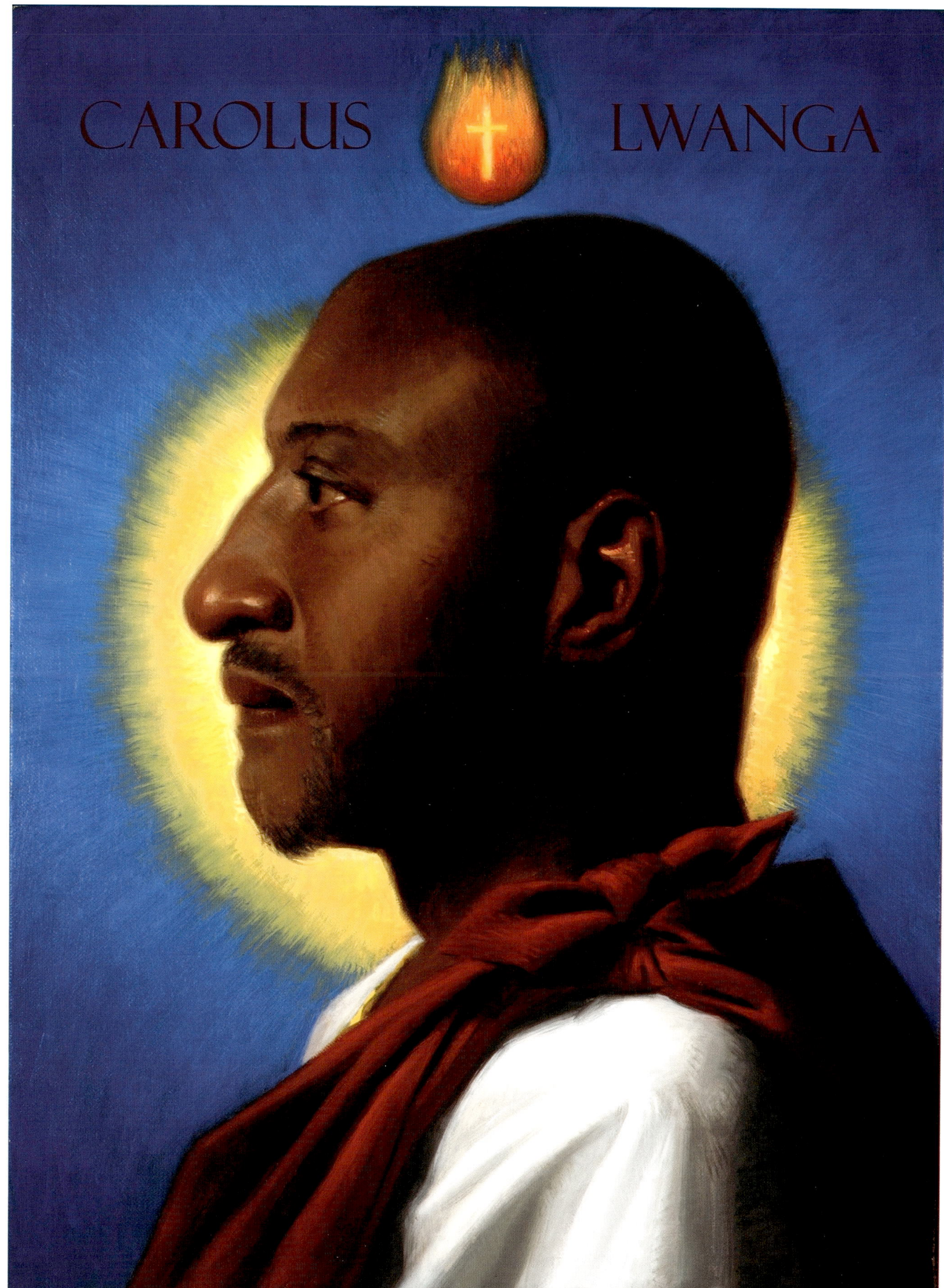
CAROLUS LWANGA

Neilson Carlin, *Saint Charles Lwanga*

Bernadette Carstensen

Bernadette Carstensen studied at the Columbus College of Art and Design and obtained a bachelor's degree in fine art and illustration. Born and raised in rural Ohio, Bernadette spent countless hours of her childhood drawing and painting. As an adult, she rediscovered the faith and naturally moved toward creating exclusively Catholic artwork. Now based in San Francisco, Bernadette is happily married and raising four children. She is grateful to have work that motivates her to grow in love for the Holy Family, the angels and saints, and is doing her best to spread the Gospel through beauty.

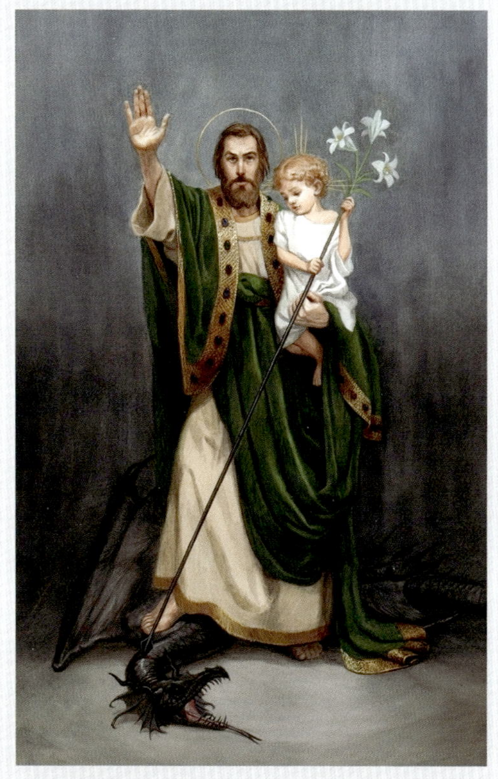

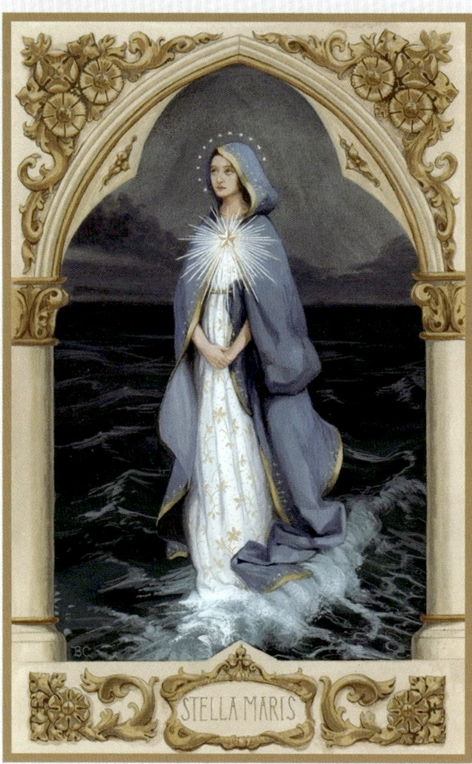

Artist's notes:

Saint Joseph Terror of Demons, 2019
Watercolor on paper

Commissioned by Father Donald Calloway in 2019 for his book *Consecration to St. Joseph*. Saint Joseph was to look strong and young, a man worthy of his protective role.

Mary Star of the Sea
Gouache on paper

A personal piece, inspired by Star of the Sea church in San Francisco and the vast, foggy ocean view that was entirely new to Bernadette.

You can find more of her work online:

www.bernadettecarstensen.com

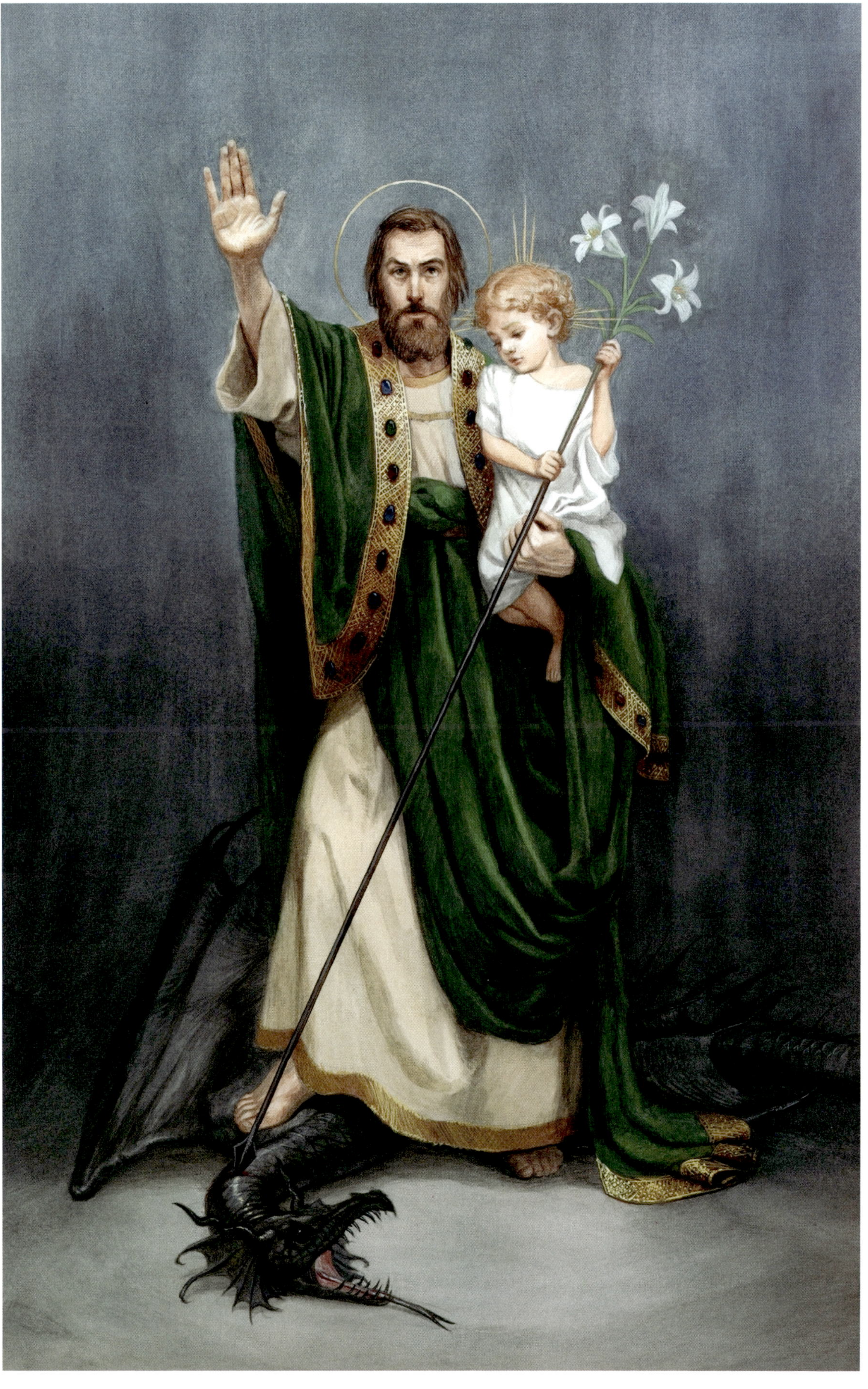

Bernadette Carstensen, *Saint Joseph Terror of Demons*, 2019
Watercolor on paper

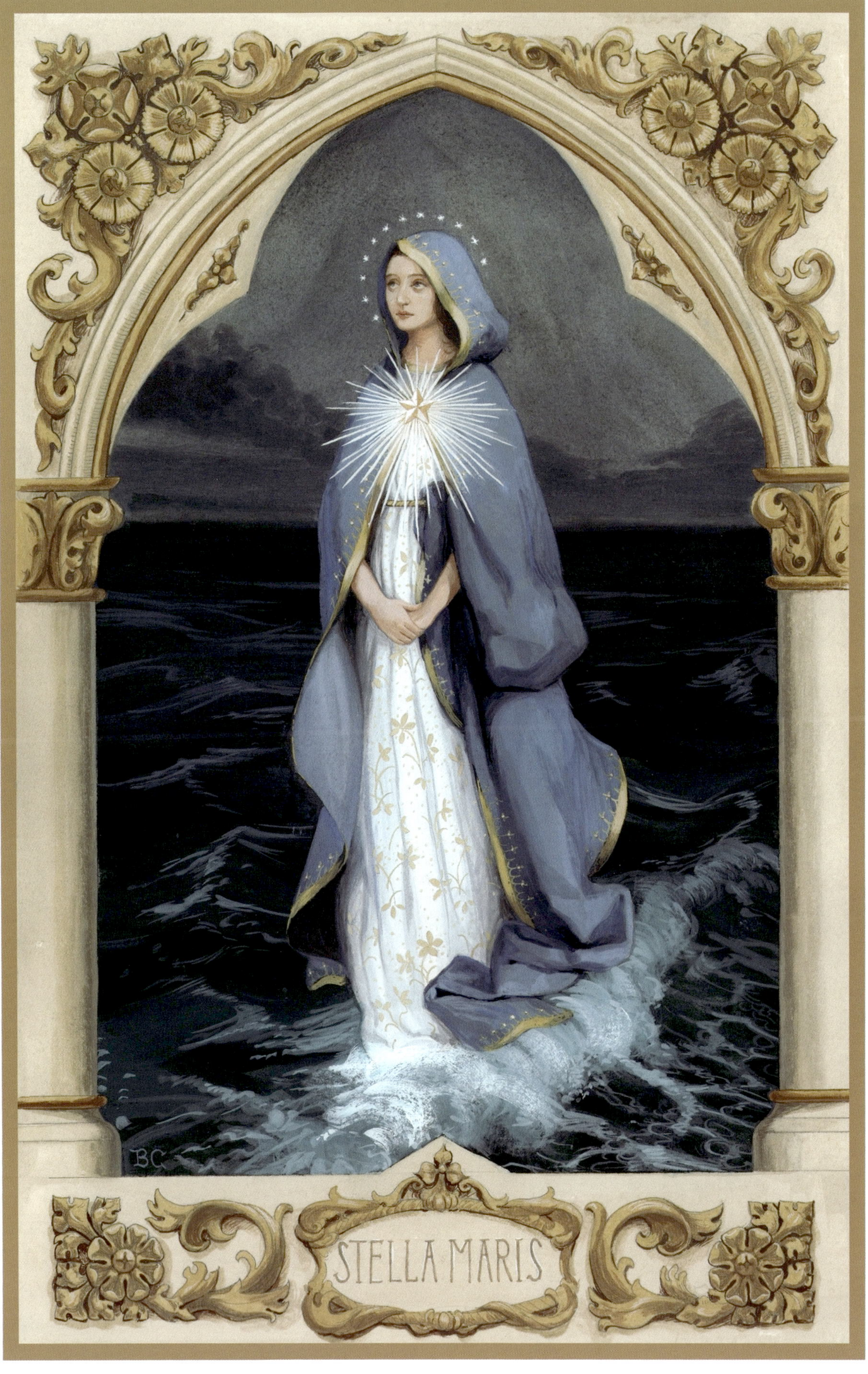
BC
STELLA MARIS

Bernadette Carstensen, *Mary Star of the Sea*
Gouache on paper

Matthew Conner

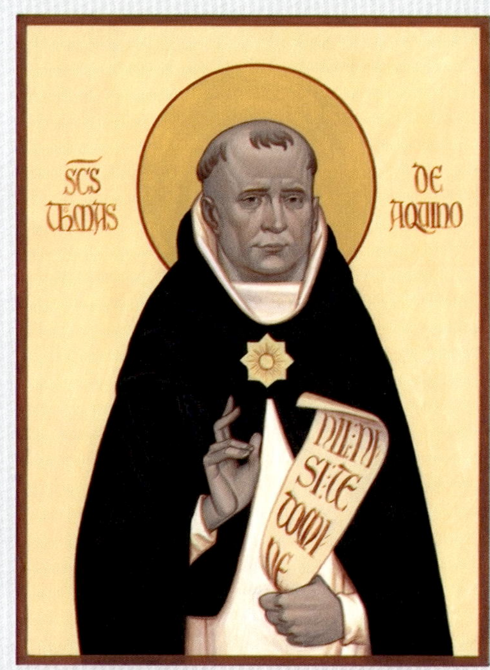

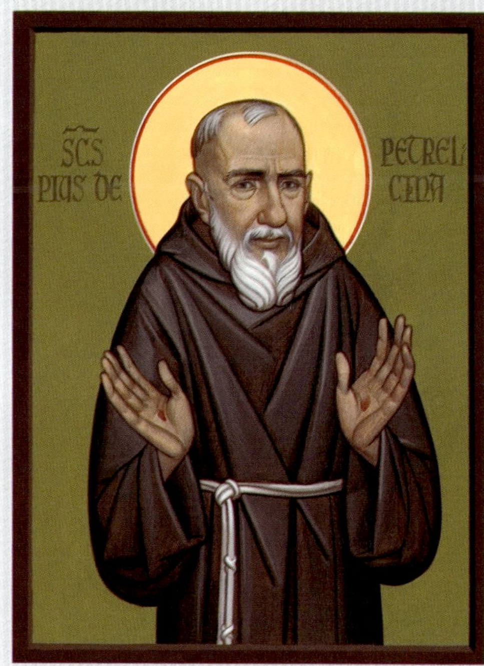

Matthew Conner studied art at the New York Academy of Art and the University of Tennessee at Chattanooga. After nearly a decade as a working artist in New York City, he returned to the South and to painting full-time.

"Saint Thomas says that God is the efficient, exemplary, and final cause of all Creation, i.e., He is its source, pattern, and ultimate purpose. So all of Creation, all that we are and all that we do, is made for this return to God. Not that He is needful of worship. Rather, He desires to share His self-perfect goodness; bonum diffusivum sui. *Likewise, art from the simplicity of a decorative design to a refreshing pastoral landscape to devotional and liturgical art ought, in various ways, to be oriented to union with our good Lord."*

— **Matthew Conner**

Artist's notes:

Saint Thomas Aquinas
Acrylic on panel, 6 x 8 in.

Saint Thomas Aquinas is known as a great scholar and teacher but was/is principally motivated by a profound love of God. When asked by Christ what he would have in reward for his labors, he answered, "*Nihil nisi te, Domine*" (Nothing but you, Lord).

Saint Padre Pio
Acrylic on panel, 6 x 8 in.

Saint Padre Pio, likewise a priest and religious, entered profoundly into the Passion of our good Lord, bearing in his body the wounds of Christ. Following his divine model, Padre Pio spent his earthly life offering these graces received to others through the sacraments of Holy Mass and confession.

Conner's work, print shop, and information about purchasing or commissioning original work can be found on his website. He is also on Instagram.

www.matthew-conner.com
Instagram: @matthaeusconner

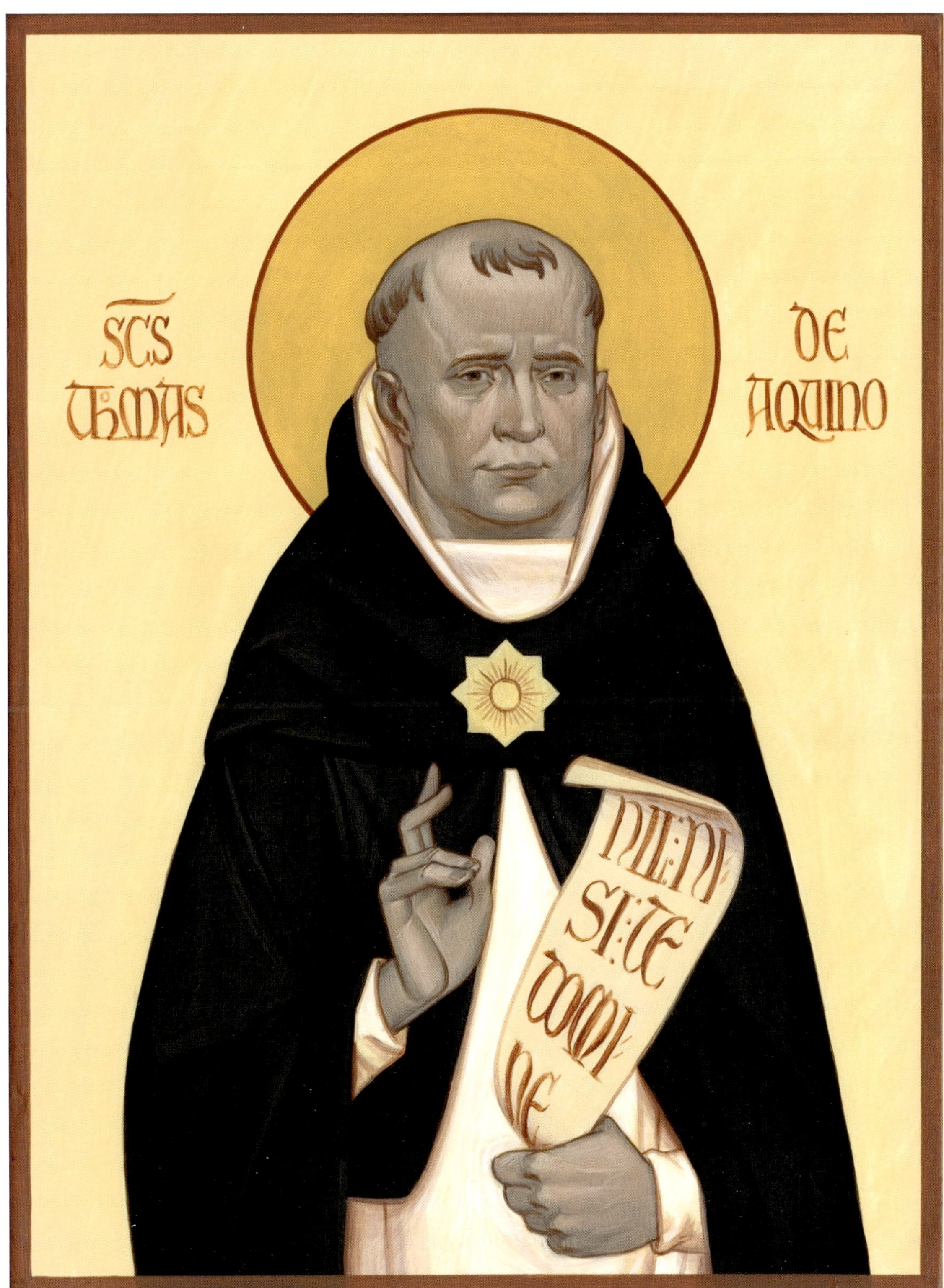
SCS
THOMAS
DE
AQUINO
NIL:NI
SI:TE
DOMI
NE

Matthew Conner, *Saint Thomas Aquinas*
Acrylic on panel, 6 x 8 in.

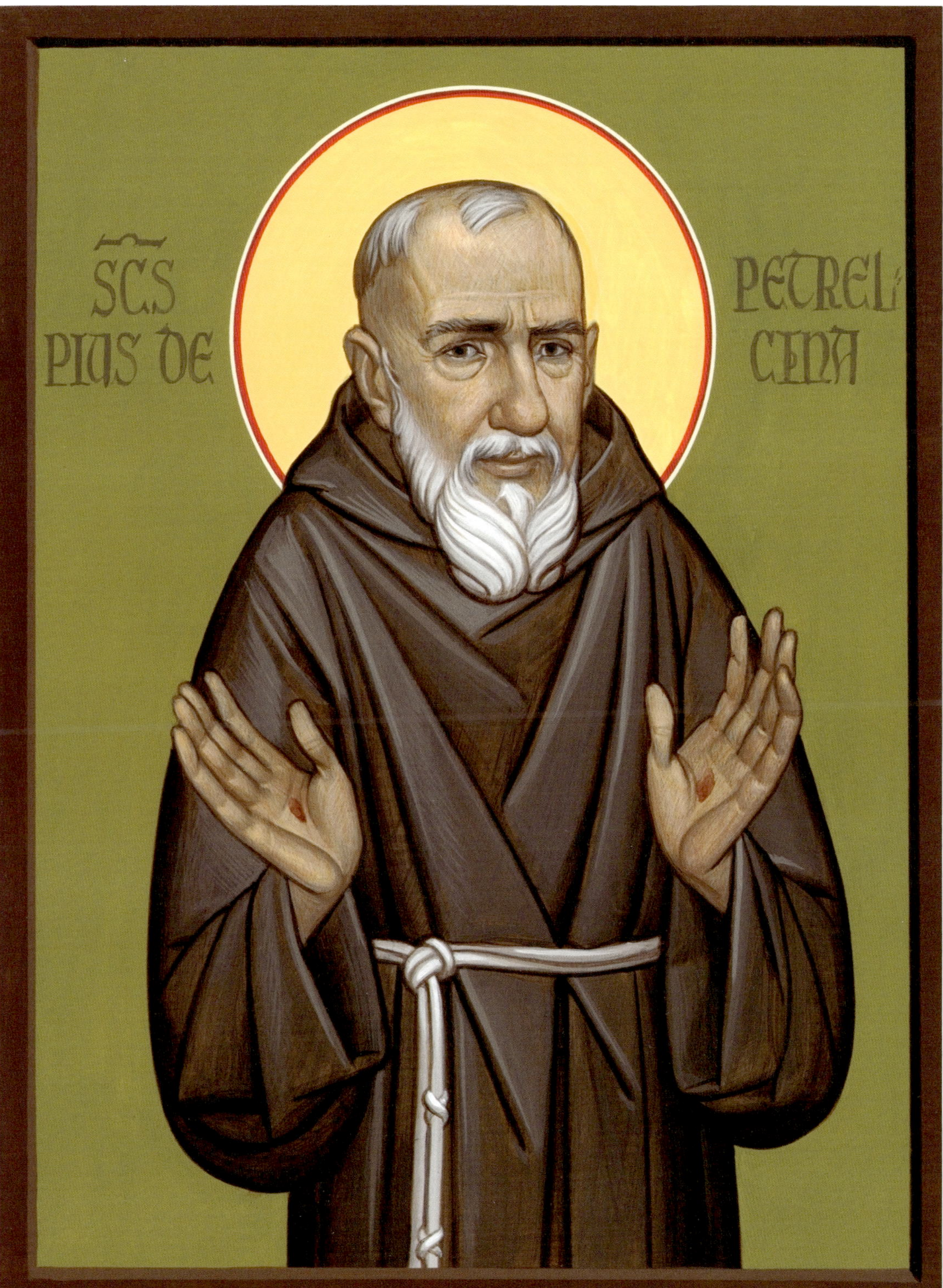
SCS
PIUS DE
PETREL
CINA

Matthew Conner, *Saint Padre Pio*
Acrylic on panel, 6 x 8 in.

James B. Janknegt

James B. Janknegt is a native Texan. Interested in art from an early age, he has a BFA in studio art from the University of Texas and an MA in printmaking and MFA in drawing and painting from the University of Iowa. He has been exhibiting his work professionally since he finished grad school, and his work is held in collections around the United States.

Faith has also been of importance to Janknegt since an early age. He says, "At one point in my life, around the year 2000, I thought to myself: my faith has been the focal point of my life since I was a teenager. Why not make my faith the focal point of my art work. Since then I have devoted myself to painting about the story of salvation. It is such a rich and deep subject, I could not exhaust it in several lifetimes."

In 2007 James and his wife entered the Catholic Church. They are very active in parish life, having led RCIA, Bible study, and music programs. He is also an active gardener and carpenter, recently building a small cottage on his property.

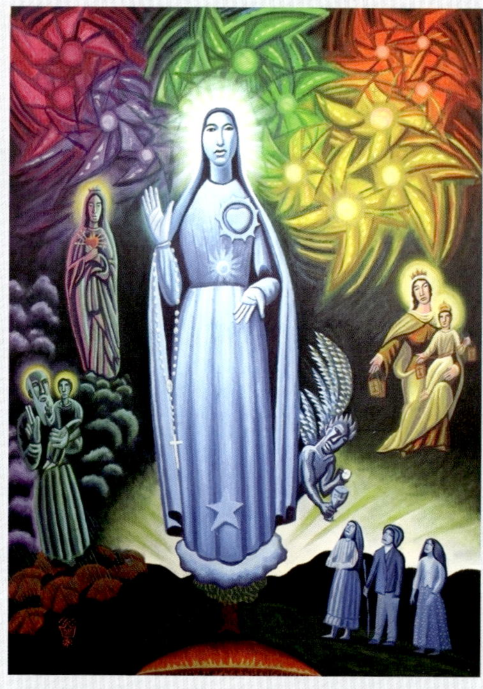

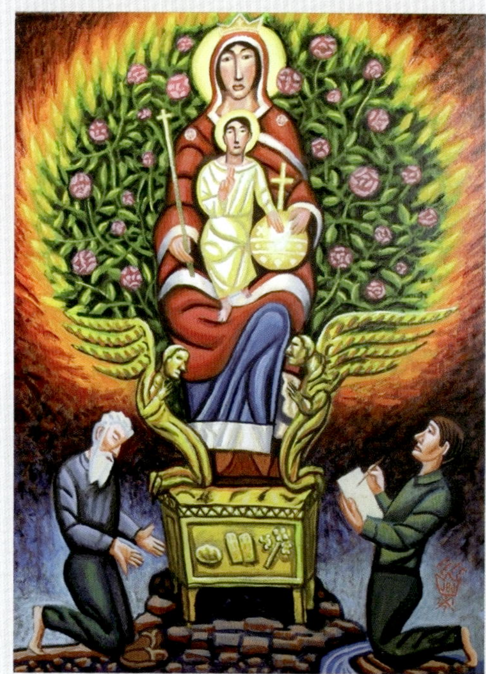

Artist's notes:

Miracle of the Sun
Oil on canvas, 30 x 40 in.

I painted this painting in honor of the 100th anniversary of Our Lady of Fatima. It depicts the culmination of her apparitions—the miracle of the sun.

Mary, the Ark
Oil on canvas, 18 x 24 in.

In this painting, I combine two beautiful appellations for Our Lady—the Ark of the Covenant and the Burning Bush. Mary is the New Ark as she held within her the Bread of Life, the Word Made Flesh, and the Great High Priest after the order of Melchizedek prefigured in the original contents of the ark of the covenant: the manna, the tablets of the Ten Commandments and Aaron's rod. Mary is like Moses in that as Moses could stand in front of God who appears as a burning bush and not be consumed, Mary could contain God in her womb and not be consumed.

You can find more of his art online or follow his work on Facebook and Instagram:

www.bcartfarm.com

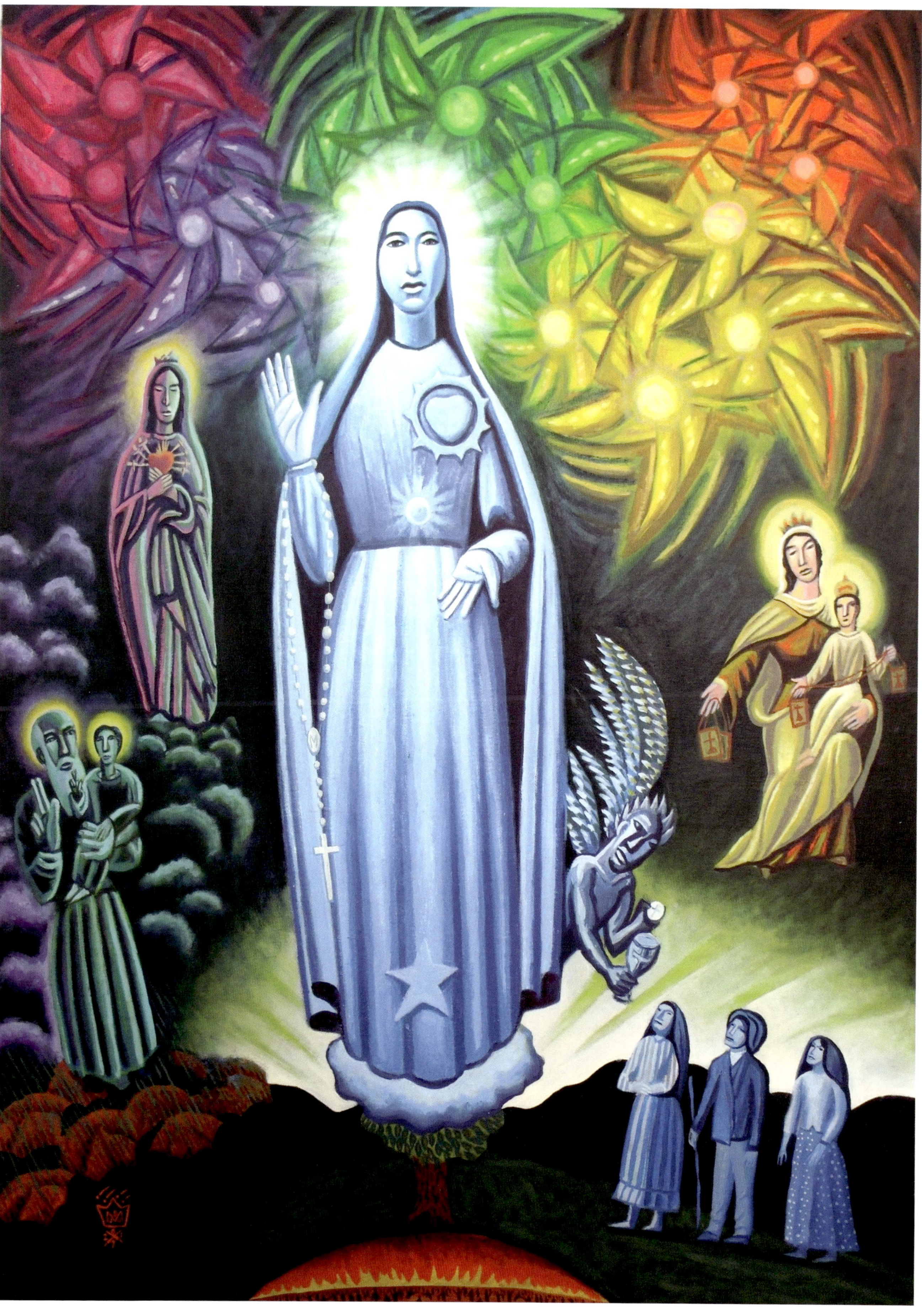

James B. Janknegt, *Miracle of the Sun*
Oil on canvas, 30 x 40 in.

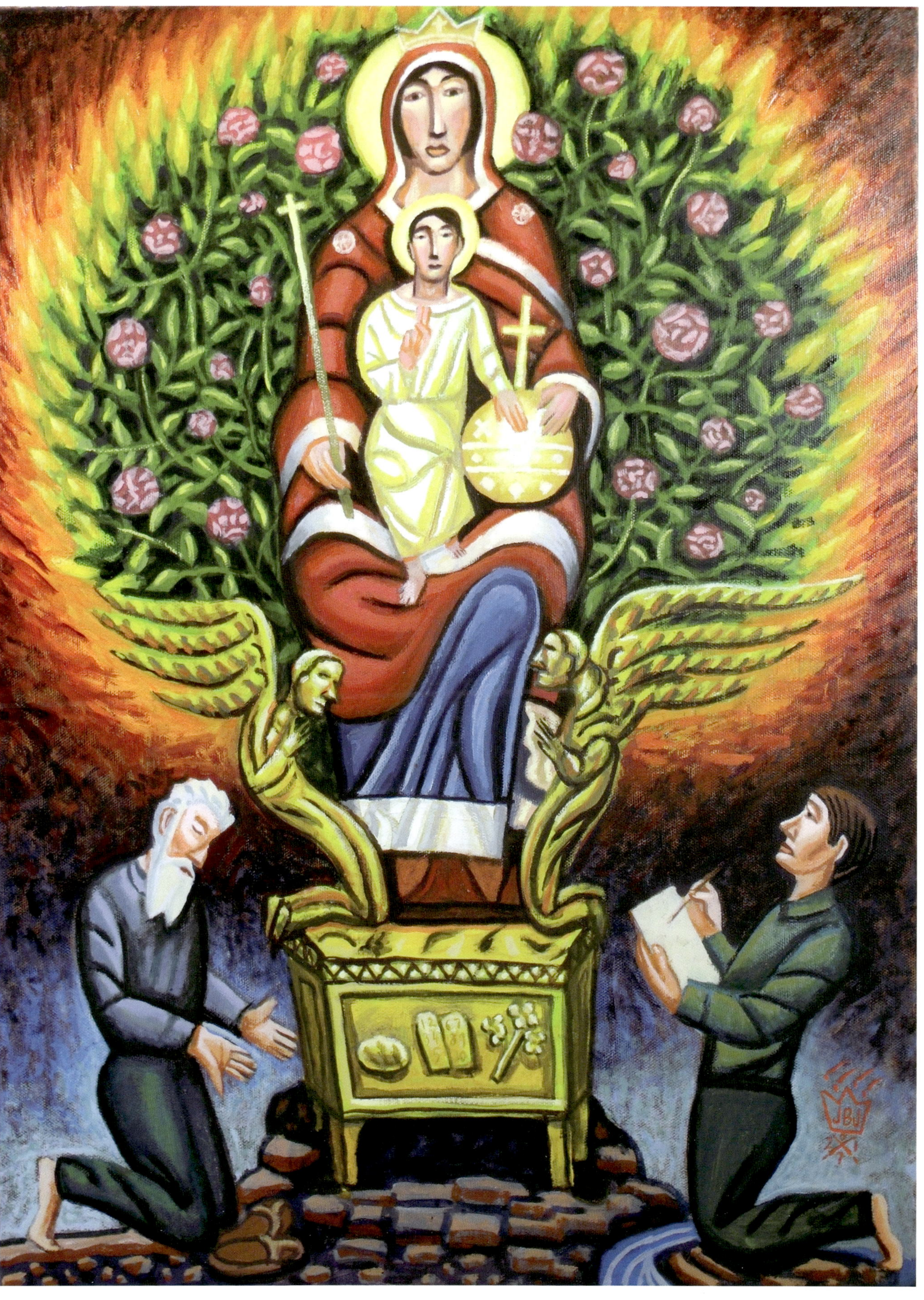

James B. Janknegt, *Mary, the Ark*
Oil on canvas, 18 x 24 in.

James B. Janknegt, *Mary, the Ark*
Oil on canvas, 18 x 24 in.

Timothy Jones

TIMOTHY JONES teaches art and art history at Chesterton Academy of the Twin Cities, where he has been part of the faculty since 2012. In addition to religious art, Jones is an accomplished painter of landscapes, nature, still-life works, and portraits. One of his previous works, a portrait of the British author G.K. Chesterton, was licensed by Ignatius Press for use on the cover of *In Defense of Sanity* (2011).

Asked how his faith informs his art, Jones says "My Catholic faith informs all of my art in some way. Many of my paintings and drawings are intended hopefully to draw the viewer's attention to the beauty of God's Creation in the most simple, ordinary things around us; a leaf or the surface of a pond."

Living in Saint Paul has also proven to be inspirational. Jones is an avid walker, and local sights have helped inform his work. "Many of my nature studies of leaves, plants, and water are inspired by long walks around my neighborhood in Saint Paul. I am also grateful to live only a few blocks from my parish church, which means I often hear the church bells and can easily walk to Mass, which is a great blessing."

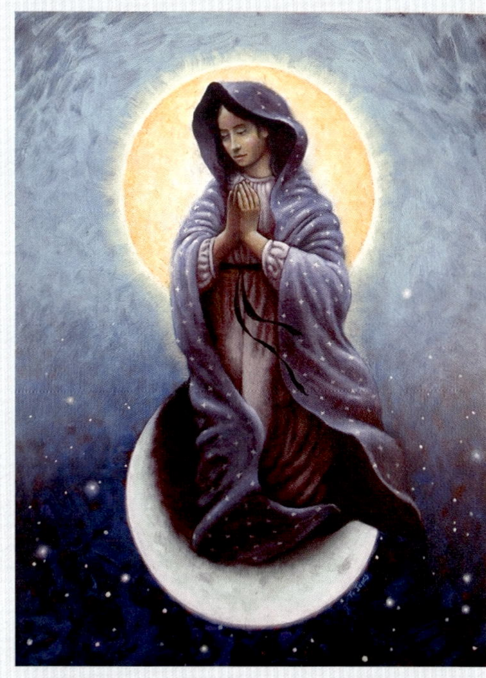

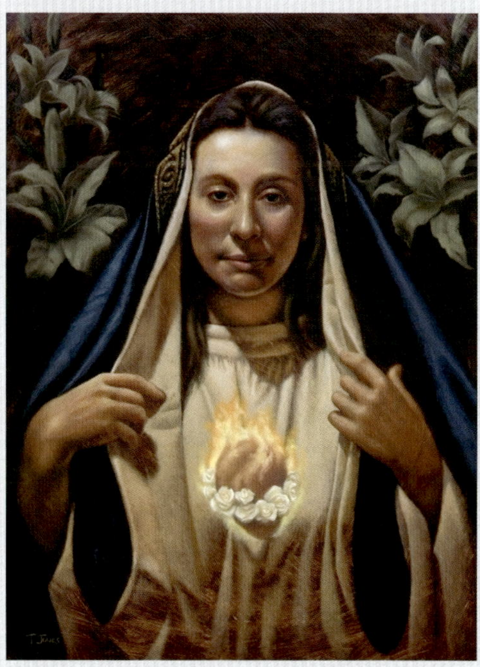

Artist's notes:

Mary, Queen of Heaven
Oils on wood panel, 12 x 16 in.

It was inspired by the passage from the Book of Revelation that refers to the "woman clothed with the sun, with the moon under her feet", as well as the image of Our Lady of Guadalupe. Visually it was conceived from my imagination, which was not my usual approach for my paintings. Our Lady's downward glance I think communicates her attentiveness to our prayers and her compassion for us.

The Immaculate Heart
Oils on wood panel, 18 x 24 in.

It was painted using a very traditional method, beginning with a monochrome underpainting and gradually adding thin layers of colored glazing. The model was a wonderful woman from my parish, who very nicely consented to pose for me. I thought she had a very kind face, and this was the aspect of Mary's character I tried to express in the image.

His online portfolio, which he hopes to expand with more specifically religious works soon, can be found online. Prints of his work in various sizes and configurations can be found at Fine Art America.

timothyjonesfineart.com
fineartamerica.com/profiles/2-timothy-jones.

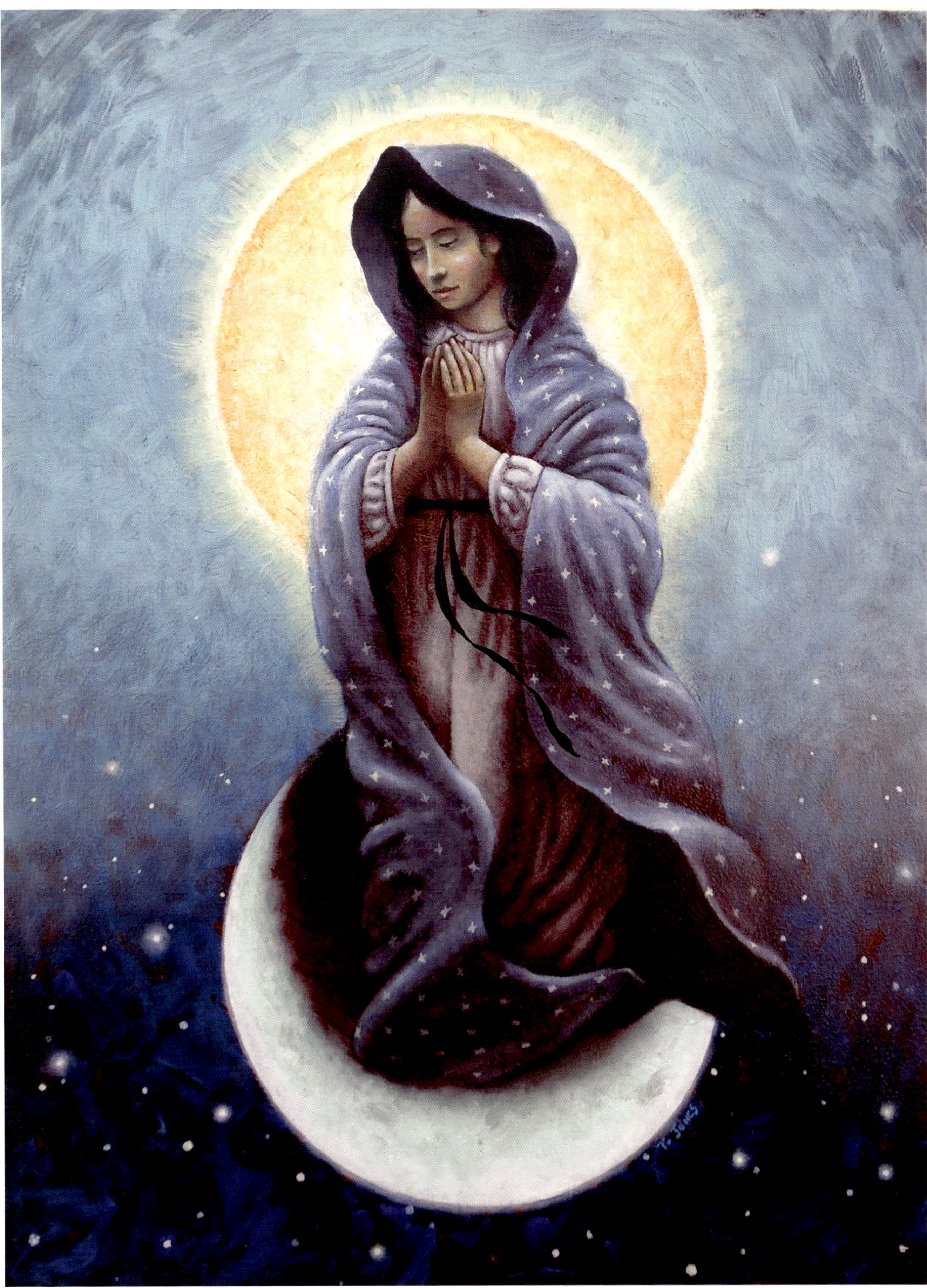
T. Jones

Timothy Jones, *Mary, Queen of Heaven*
Oils on wood panel, 12 x 16 in.

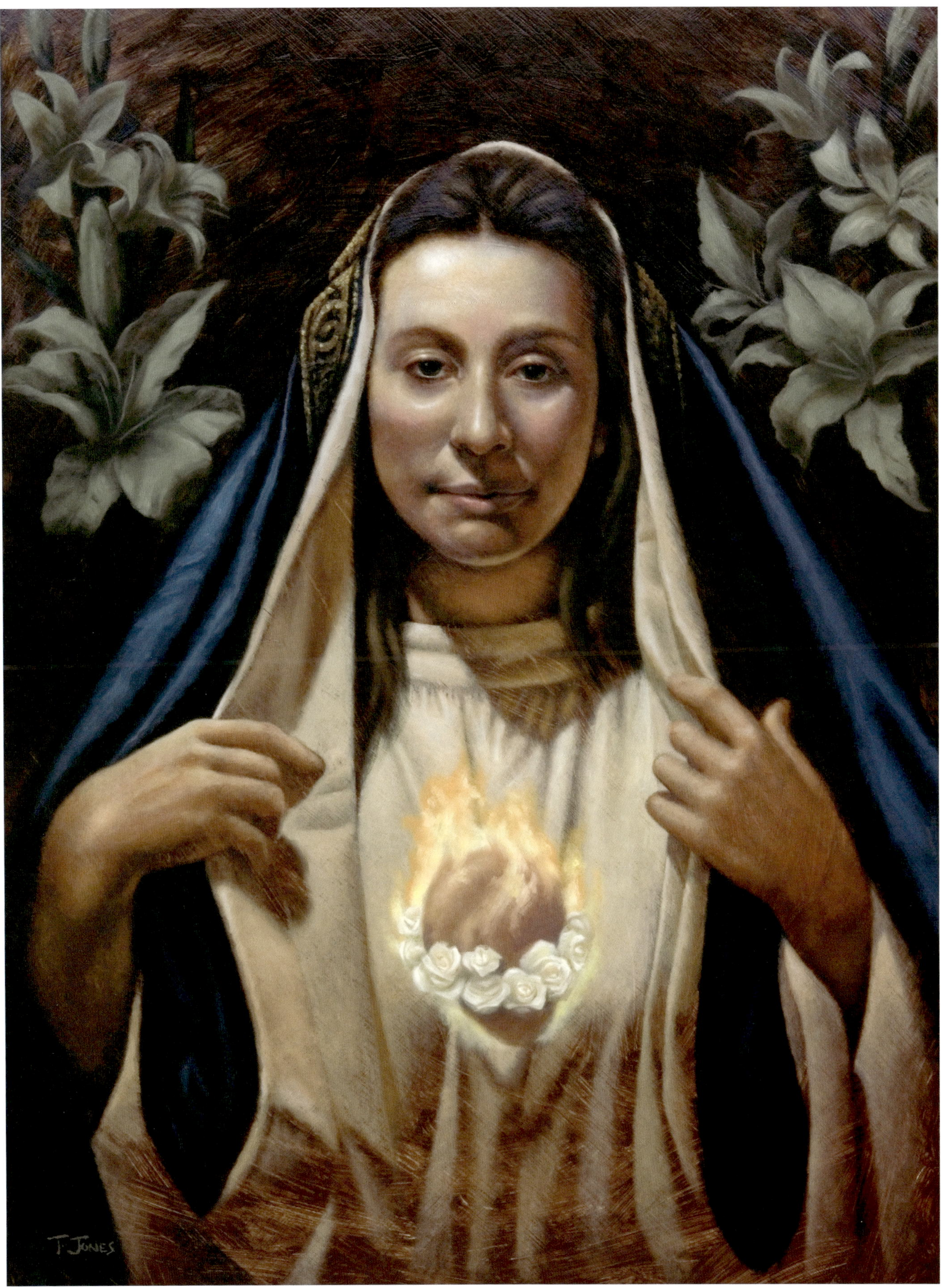
T. JONES

Timothy Jones, *The Immaculate Heart*
Oils on wood panel, 18 x 24 in.

Michael D. O'Brien

Michael D. O'Brien is known to countless readers as one of the preeminent Catholic novelists of our time. In addition to his writing, he has been a working artist since 1970, with his works in many collections around the world. His paintings have been featured on the covers of his novels, and a recent book, *The Art of Michael O'Brien,* is a major work focusing on the entirety of his artistic career.

In addition to his novels, Michael O'Brien has written many essays of cultural and literary criticism, has contributed to Catholic magazines and newspapers, and has spoken at conferences around the world. He lives in northern Ontario with his wife, Sheila.

"It is absolutely essential that we submit ourselves to a discipline, and in this I think we can do no better than learn from the masters in all the arts who have gone before us. I am also convinced that one must not pay much attention to the current social standards in both painting and writing. Modern cultural norms are dominated by a philosophical revolution that is intent on removing the sacred and the human (I mean the whole truth about mankind) from life, and thus they cannot be trusted."

— **Michael O'Brien,**
from his "Open Letter to Fellow Writers and Artists"

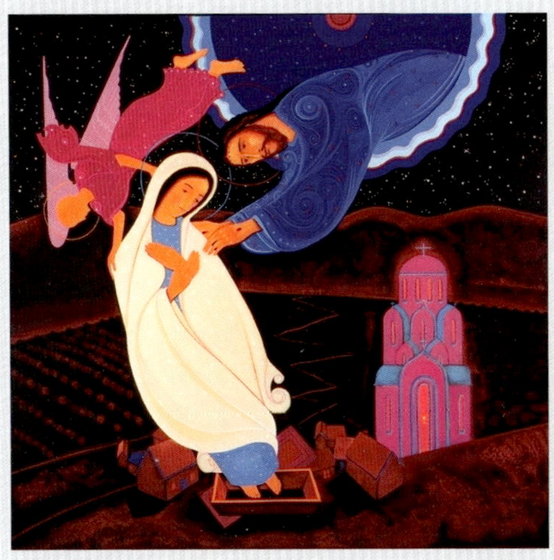

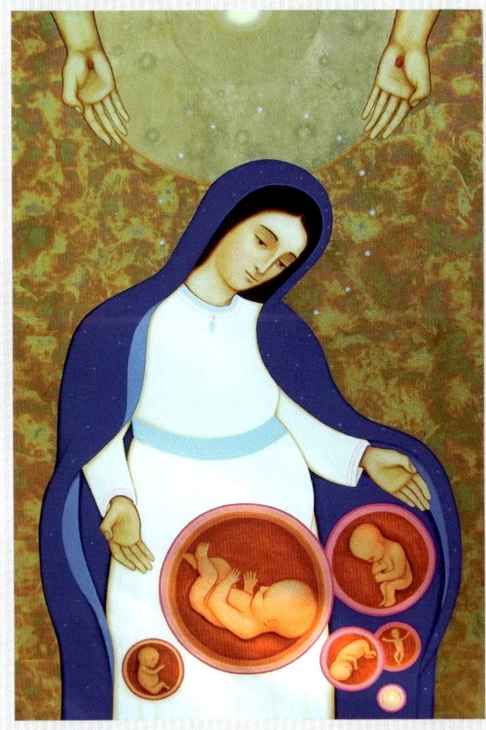

Artist's notes:

The Assumption of the Blessed Virgin Mary, 1990

In this depiction of the Assumption of Mary into Heaven, the perspective is from the sky, looking down on an ordinary village of our own times. In the background are orchards and hills and a starry night, with a road illuminated by the light from the figure of the Blessed Virgin. The road leads to and from the Cross, indicating that the mystery of the Assumption has its origins in the Passion and death of Jesus. Jesus himself, now resurrected, opens a portal in the heavens and reaches down to receive her, body and soul, assisted by an angel. Even as she is taken up, the gaze of Mary passes through the Cross to the church building symbolic of the universal Church and, finally, to the presence of Christ with us in the Blessed Sacrament. As with her Son, her presence, love, and intercession remain always with us.

Mary, the Mother of Life, 2013

Mary is given to us as a New Eve, who in her choice for the Father's will, her humble obedience, replaces the original sin committed by Eve in the Garden of Eden. Mary thus becomes the new "mother of all the living". She is depicted here as pregnant, in a form similar to that of Our Lady of Guadalupe. Her arms are open wide to offer the Son in her womb to the world, while at the same time interceding for all children in the womb at various stages of development. So, too, she receives into her hands the souls of those innocents who are slaughtered through abortion. The twelve stars crowning her head indicate that she is the Woman clothed with the sun in the book of Revelation 12, she who will crush the head of the serpent who brought death and falsehood into the world.

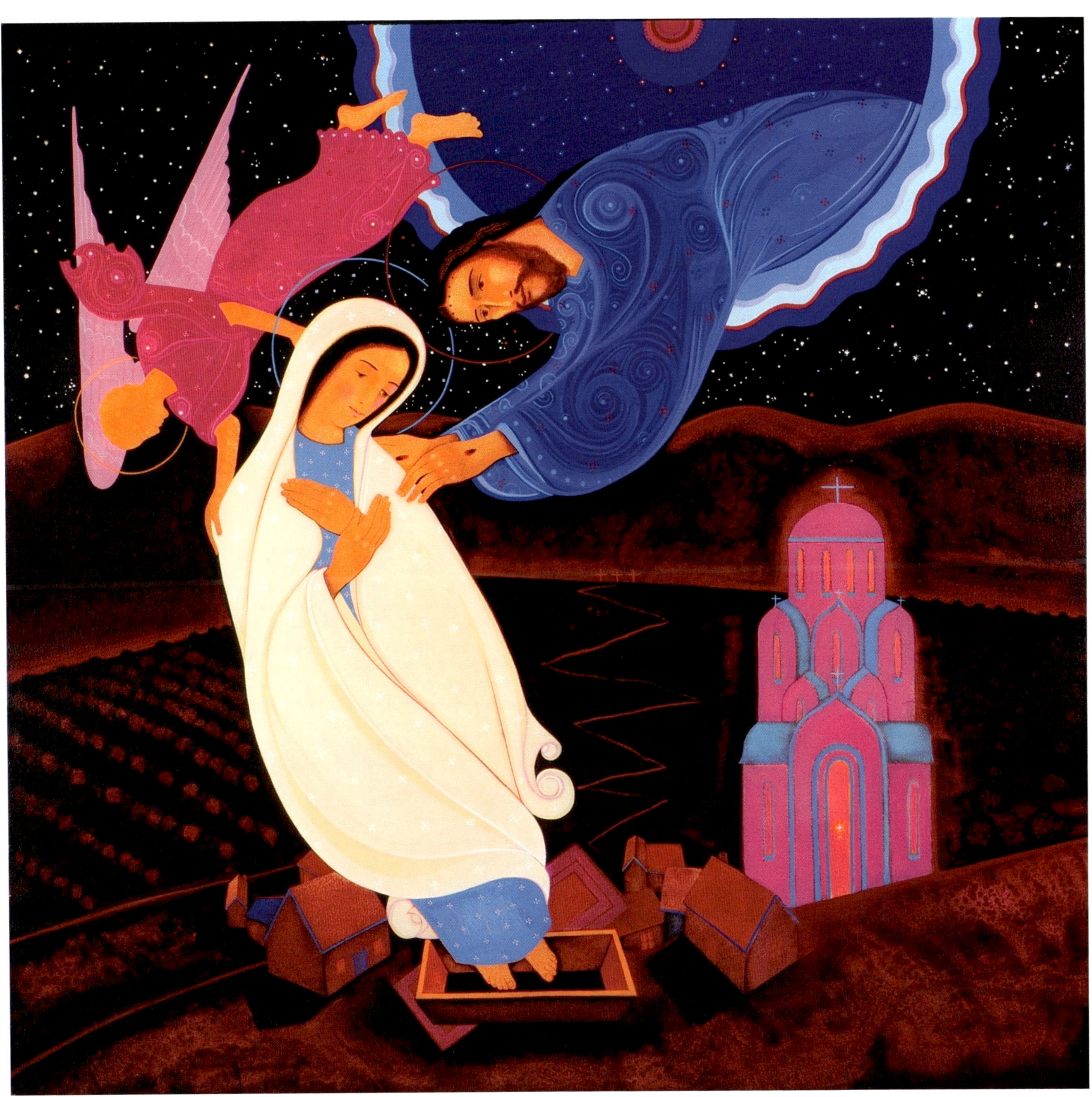

Michael D. O'Brien, *The Assumption of the Blessed Virgin Mary*, 1990

Michael D. O'Brien, *The Assumption of the Blessed Virgin Mary*, 1990

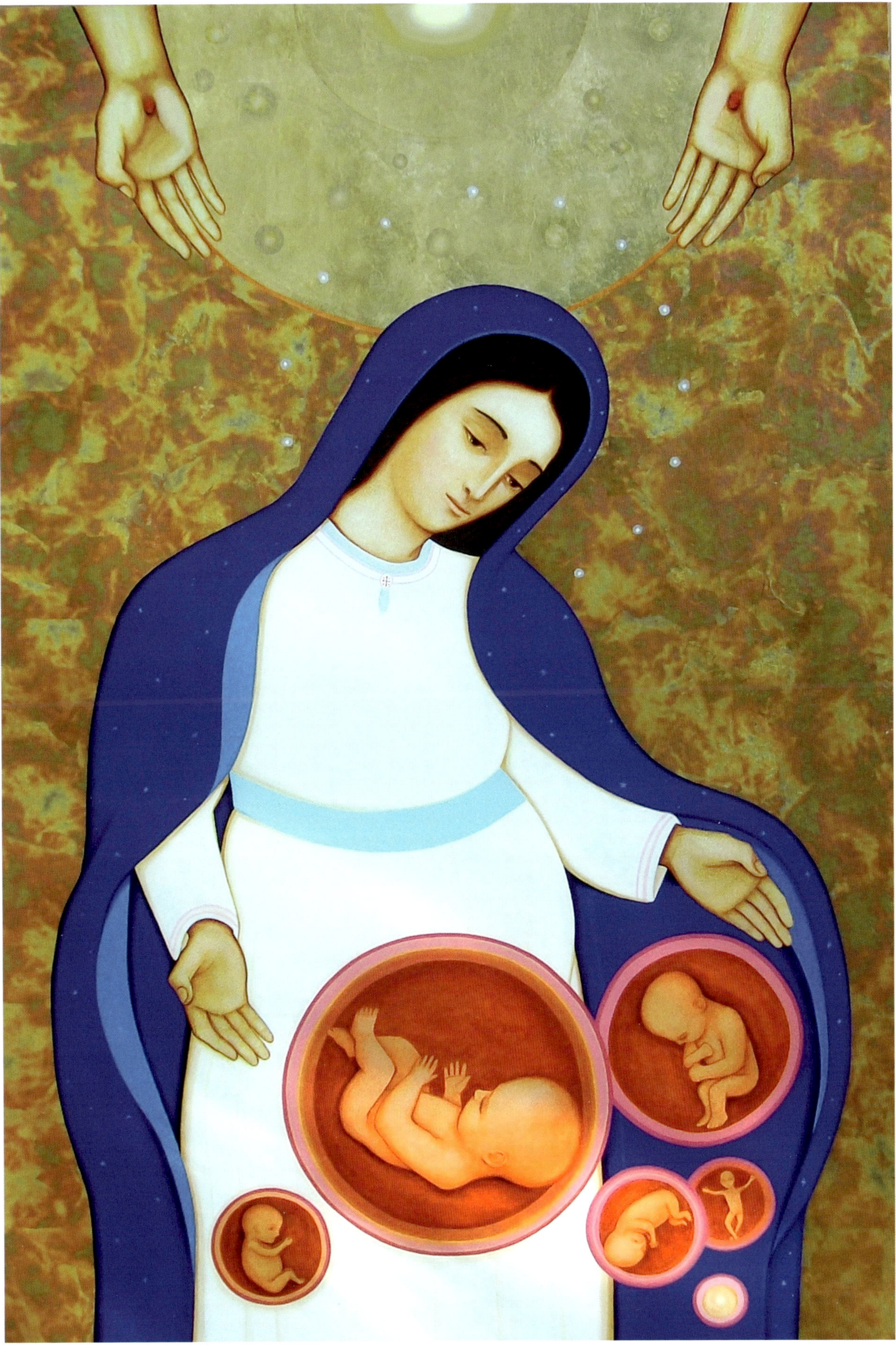

Michael D. O'Brien, *Mary, the Mother of Life,* 2013

Gwyneth Thompson-Briggs

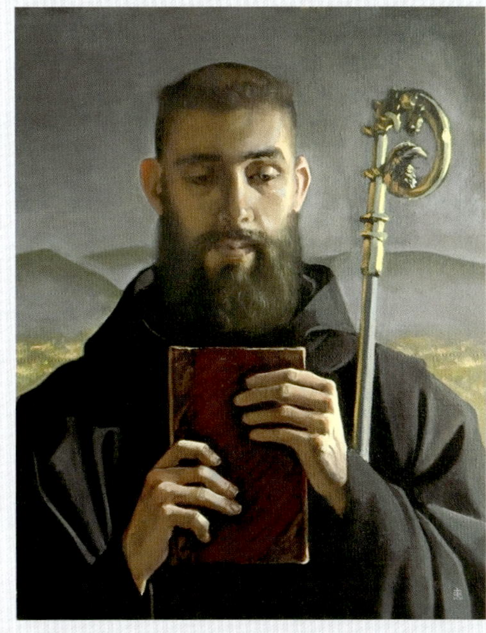

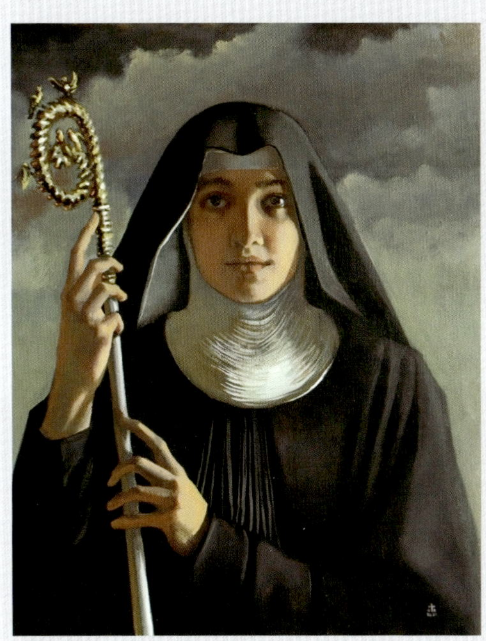

GWYNETH THOMPSON-BRIGGS studied under Tony Ortega at the Art Students League of Denver and went on to earn a BFA at the Rocky Mountain College of Art and Design. She also holds advanced degrees in Physics and Engineering and was Visiting Fellow and Artist-in-Residence at Thomas More College of Liberal Arts in New Hampshire, where she and her husband developed a course on sacred art theory and practice.

Specializing in the techniques of the Renaissance and Baroque eras, Gwyneth says, "The great Renaissance and Baroque artists paid painstaking attention to the visible world because they understood that it is through the visible that we come to know the invisible." She adds, "Restoring the beauty of worship is first of all a duty to God and an expression of our love for Him. Secondly, the patronage and creation of sacred art is an act of charity toward our neighbor, since true beauty is a reflection of God and leads us back to Him."

In 2017, Gwyneth was asked to create a painting for Pope Emeritus Benedict XVI, and in 2019 she founded the Catholic Artists Directory, helping connect artists and patrons of sacred art.

She resides in St. Louis, Mo., with her husband, Andrew, and three children.

Artist's notes:

St. Benedict and ***St. Scholastica***, 2020
Oil on linen, 65 cm x 50.5 cm (approx. 25.5 x 20 in.)
Twin altarpieces, Monastero di San Benedetto in Monte, Norcia, Italy

Visual reference points for the twin saints requested by the monks included Charlton Heston for Benedict and—for Scholastica—Grace Kelly, Sophia Loren, and Julia Child. Painted from sibling models in a glow at once Umbrian and celestial, the images are meant to complement the whispers of private Masses and prayer.

Gwyneth Thompson-Briggs' portfolio, information about her work, and original pieces for sale can be found at her website:

www.gwynethompsonbriggs.com

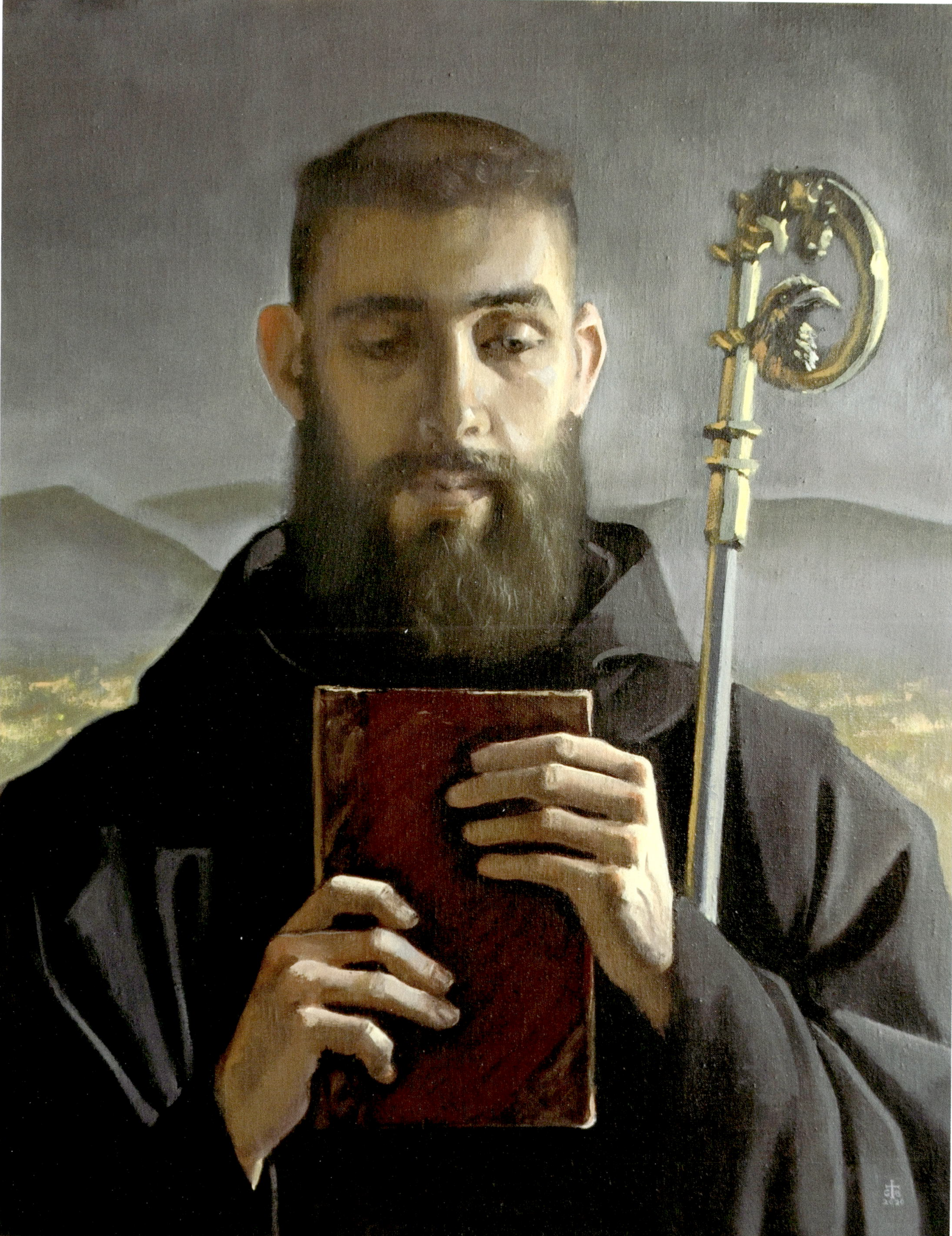

Gwyneth Thompson-Briggs, *St. Benedict*, 2020
Oil on linen, 65 cm x 50.5 cm (approx. 25.5 x 20 in.)
Monastero di San Benedetto in Monte, Norcia, Italy

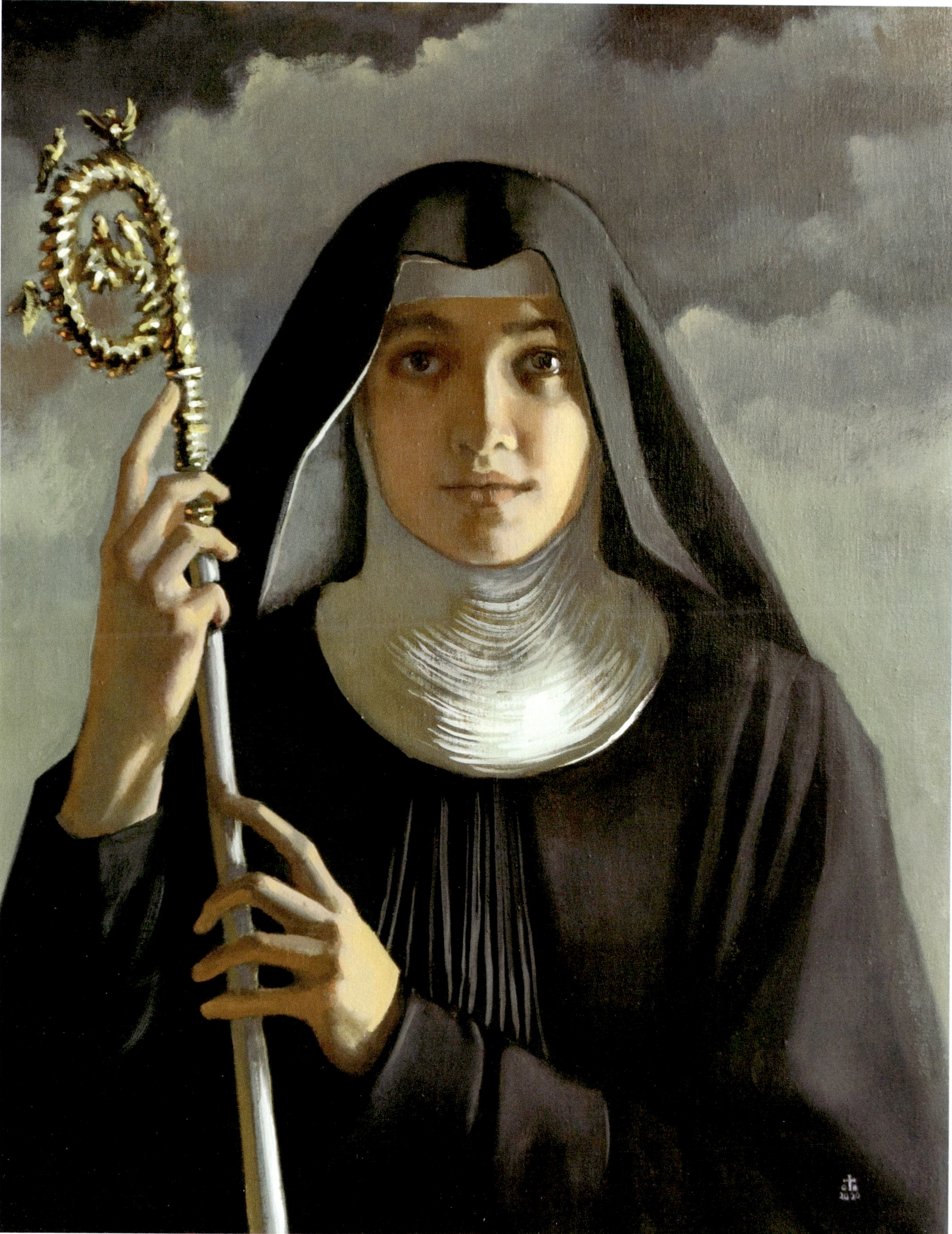

Gwyneth Thompson-Briggs, *St. Scholastica*, 2020
Oil on linen, 65 cm x 50.5 cm (approx. 25.5 x 20 in.)
Monastero di San Benedetto in Monte, Norcia, Italy

Elizabeth Zelasko

Elizabeth Zelasko grew up in New Jersey, attended the School of Visual Arts and the Prosopon School of Iconology in New York City, and later obtained a bachelor's degree at the Rocky Mountain College of Art and Design in Denver, Colorado. An early home environment provided artistic encouragement, as did her artist mother.

"Even as an undergrad working in secular themes, my faith was always what inspired my work", Zelasko says. "Praying the Liturgy of the Hours and mulling over the psalms, there was an endless reservoir of poetic imagery to pull from. Now that I primarily work in sacred art, faith plays an even greater role in my work. I find that the level of prayer and commitment to the methodology has steadily deepened my faith."

Elizabeth Zelasko's work has been featured on television and in print in many venues, including EWTN, FORMED, *National Catholic Register*, *The Denver Catholic*, *Real Life Catholic*, the Augustine Institute, the *Do Something Beautiful* Podcast with Leah Darrow, and the Catholic Radio Network.

"As an artist, I believe it is of the utmost importance to deliver my very best—the highest quality of work and materials, and passion in everything I complete. I do this work to add beauty to the Church and to peoples' homes and to elevate our minds to things above. I get lost in my work, but I pray that you find your way by contemplating the images I present. May they inspire your prayer time, cultivate silence in your heart, and enrich your homes and churches."

— **Elizabeth Zelasko**

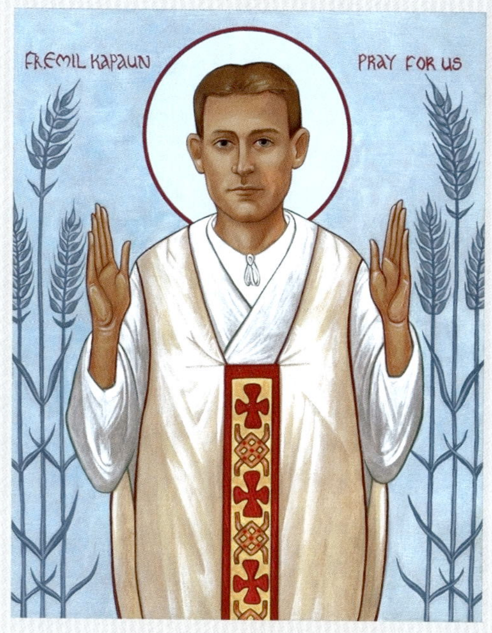

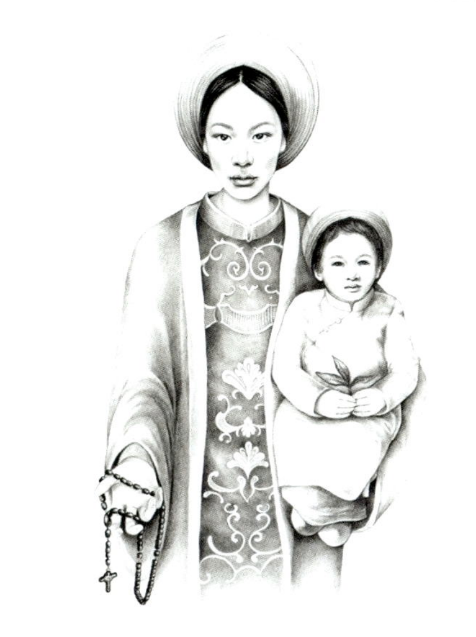

Artist's notes:

Servant of God Father Emil Kapaun
Acrylic paint on wood

Servant of God, Father Emil Kapaun is the most decorated Military Chaplain in American history. He is on his way to sainthood, and if you read his full story, you will quickly find out why.

The wheat in this icon represents both his home state of Kansas and the fulfillment of his priestly vocation. His body was truly crushed by his enemies, but his spirit was made so strong in his tribulations that he became bread for others.

Our Lady of La Vang
Graphite on paper

In 1798, the practice of Catholicism was severely restricted in Vietnam, and incredible persecution ensued for the faithful living there. Many people fled into the jungle for refuge, but poor living conditions quickly led to illness. The community gathered at the foot of a tree every evening to pray the rosary, and it was there that *Our Lady of La Vang* appeared to her persecuted children. She told them to boil the leaves of a nearby plant to cure their illness. They followed her direction, and the illness disappeared from their community.

In my version of the apparition we see the Infant Jesus holding this healing leaf in His hands. Mary appeared to the people in traditional Vietnamese garments showing them that she was one of them, their mother.

Đức Mẹ La Vang is very important to the Vietnamese people today. Let us continue to pray with and for the persecuted, displaced, and marginalized Christians throughout the world. May their adherence to the faith not go unnoticed but, instead, be used as salt for the earth.

Elizabeth Zelasko's online portfolio and print shop can be found online and on Instagram.

elizabethzelasko.com
Instagram: @elizabeth.zelasko
Email: eliza.bethzelaskoart@gmail.com

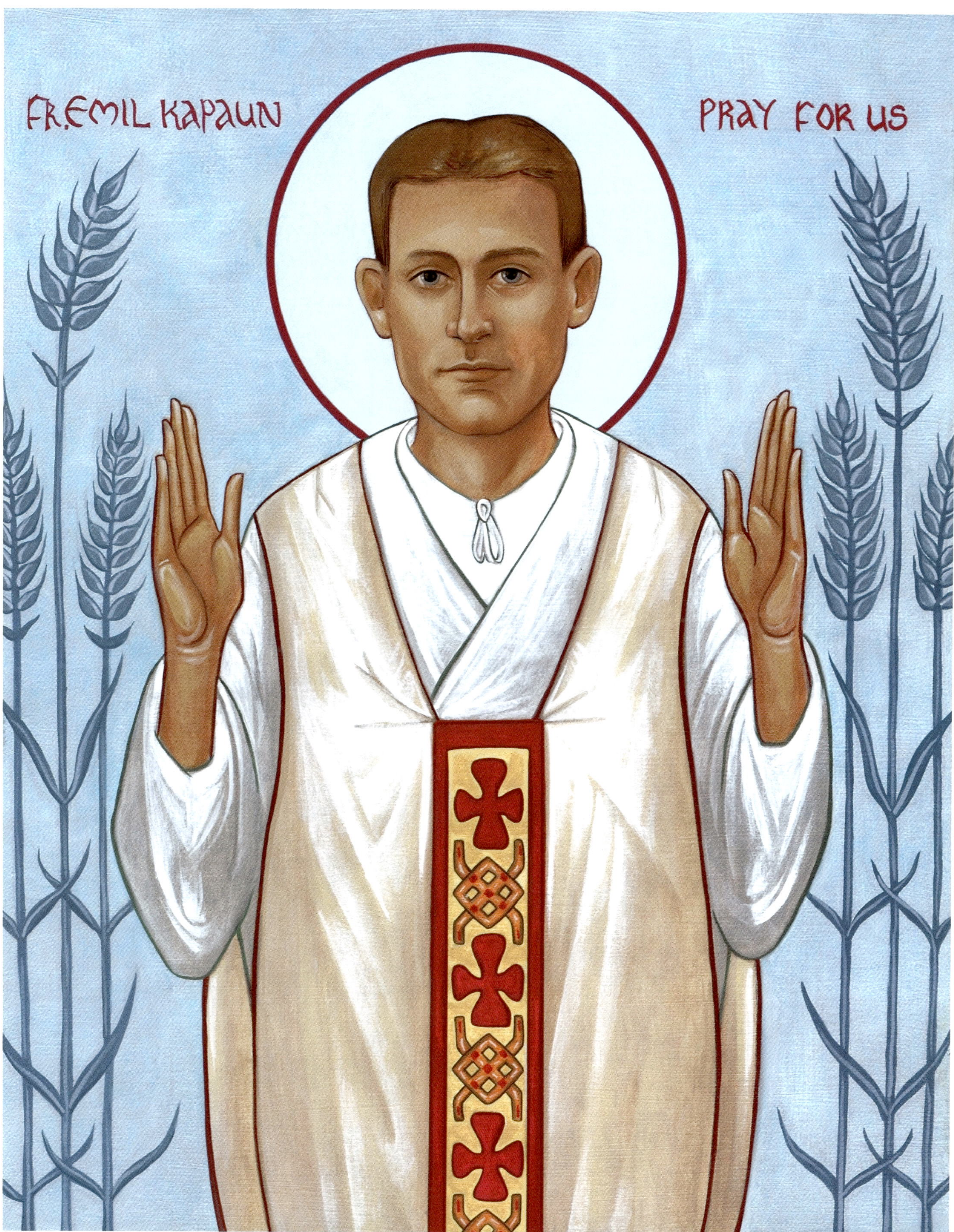
Fr. Emil Kapaun
Pray for us

Elizabeth Zelasko, *Servant of God Father Emil Kapaun*
Acrylic paint on wood

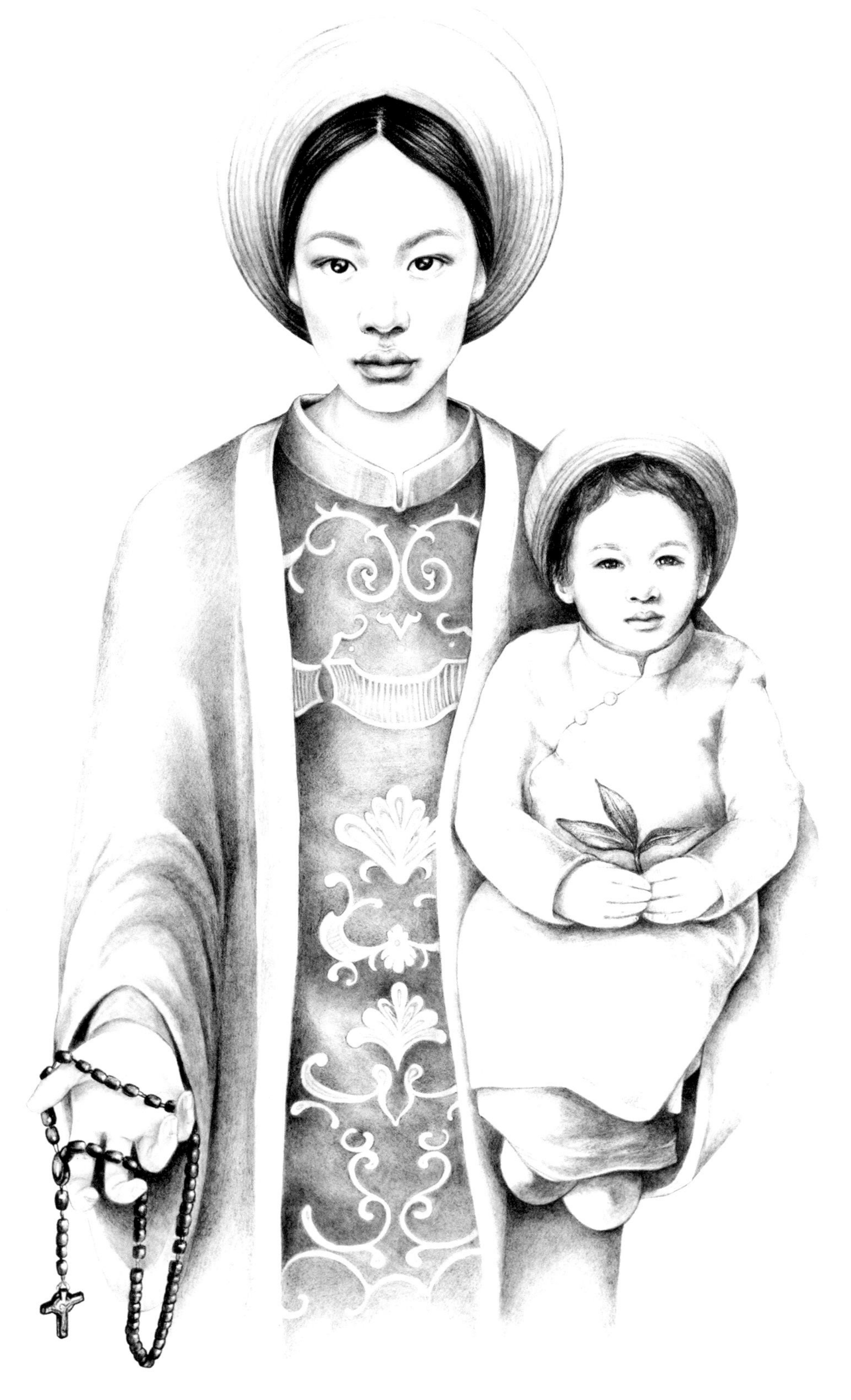

Elizabeth Zelasko, *Our Lady of La Vang*
Graphite on paper

A Note from the Editor

Over the years I have collected various folios of prints and bound volumes featuring reproductions of artwork, mostly from the early twentieth century. These collections introduced me to artists with whom I was until then unfamiliar, many of whom have now become favorites.

So why this new folio of prints? In conversations with friends, I kept hearing people say such things as "I wish we had great Catholic artists working today." The thing is, we do! But with the overload of information in the digital age, it is often difficult to find these artists if you don't know where to look. An old-fashioned solution came to mind: a modern version of a folio book, with prints that can be removed and framed. At a certain point, I gathered together images from artists I knew of and presented the idea to the editors at Ignatius Press. It took another few years to get the project rolling, but here it is!

My first hope for this little gallery is that it will prompt you to visit these artists online, learn more about their work—maybe even patronize them by buying original work from them directly.

My second hope is that this little gallery is popular enough that a second, third, fourth, or maybe even fifth edition could be published, gathering together even more currently working Catholic artists.

Beato Angelico (Blessed John of Fiesole, O.P.), pray for us, and pray for our Catholic artists!

John Herreid